Voidworking

Practical Sorcery from Primordial Nothingness

Voidworking

Practical Sorcery from Primordial Nothingness

Dave Smith

Stafford, UK

Voidworking: Practical Sorcery from Primordial Nothingness
Dave Smith © 2020

All rights reserved, including the right to reproduce this book, or portions thereof, in any form.

The right of Dave Smith to be identified as the author of this work has been asserted by him in accordance with the Copyright, Designs and Patents Act, 1988.

Editor: Storm Constantine
Cover Art and Design: Danielle Lainton

ISBN: 978-1-912241-17-0
Catalogue Number: MB0209

Set in Book Antiqua

Megalithica Books Edition 2020
www.immanion-press.com
info@immanion-press.com

This book is dedicated to Typhon Draconis, who left this world and passed back into the Void in July of 2019. He was a friend and a tireless supporter of my work.

Contents

Introduction – What is the Void?	9
Caveats	14
Part I: Laying the Foundation	19
Religion and Cosmology	19
Philosophy	25
Contemporary Magic	28
Popular Culture	32
Fiction	33
Music	36
Video Games	37
Film	38
Part II: Voidworking	40
What is Magic?	42
Why Do Magic?	45
Tuning the Magical Mind	49
Re-Imagining the Self	56
The Nature and Use of Ritual	58
The Importance of Symbols	64
Symbolizing the Self	66
The Glyph of the Void	67
The Primal Vortex	68
Emanations of the Void	70
Gods and Monsters	73
Visualization	77

Voidworking in Practice	78
Tools, Trappings, and Correspondences	79
Void Stones	81
Black Water	83
Hallowing	84
Banishing	85
Meditating on the Void	90
Disintegration	93
The Rite of Erasure	94
The Black Jar	97
Black Ice	99
Deep Diving	100
Distilling the Static	104
The Veil of Shadows	107
Scrying: Gazing into the Void	108
The Last: Contemplating Death	111
Conclusion	115
Sources consulted	117
About the Author	122

Introduction
What is the Void?

Do you *know* Nothing? If you don't, you will, inasmuch as it can be known. When I first discussed this project with a friend, he asked what is there possibly to say about the Void? That's a fair question. It's not a topic that seems to have a great deal of approachability. However, through the investigation of various sources and conceptions, this work is intended to provide a thorough, practical understanding of what the Void is, and how its power and potential can be used in magical workings of various kinds.

The concept of the Void itself is one that most occultists are likely familiar with but may not have spent much effort contemplating. It is mentioned briefly in works that too often seem to assume that the reader has a thorough understanding of the concept and its aspects and applications, but such an understanding is difficult to acquire. Where is the entry point to this information? There is a wide variety of material on the subject, but it is scattered through magical, religious, philosophical, and scientific works of numerous cultures and eras. These sources are further enriched by a deep body of contemporary fictional treatments of the Void in written literature and video games.

I've long been both fascinated and discomfited by the idea of nothingness. It seems natural to abhor it, yet throughout the progression of my practice, in each of the paradigms and faiths that I have worked in, I've always looked for how each one addressed the concept. In English, it is variously called the Void (from the Latin *vacare*, or vacate via Old French), the Abyss (from the Greek *abussos*, or bottomless), or simply Nothingness. Throughout this work I will use whichever term is representative of the source material that I'm discussing, although in my own nomenclature, I refer to it as the *Void*, capitalized as a proper name.

The first question to answer, is what exactly do I mean by the Void? Is it a physical place? Is it a metaphysical concept? Is it a state of consciousness? Much like the term *chaos*, with which it is often interchangeable, it has many meanings. It is each of these things and more. Just as Lao Tzu wrote that the *Dao* that can be described in words is not the true *Dao*, and Austin Spare held that the *Kia* which can be expressed by conceivable ideas is not the eternal *Kia*, conceptualizing the Void is inherently elusive. It defies a single strict definition.

A workable place to begin with is that the Void is the inverse of that which *is*. It represents a state of existence that has not yet been ordered by a sentient force, nor metamorphosed into another state of being via some process of self-organization. It is emptiness without bounds or limits. It is this state from whence we come, and to which we shall return, and among most people it is a source of dread. We cannot experience the Void directly through our physical senses, but we can visualize it and contemplate it in our minds. Semantically, it is a blank canvas onto which intent can be layered, and the seeds of Will planted in order to achieve desired results. It is simultaneously sheer simplicity and infinite potential. It is not Hell or purgatory, for it predates the conception of either.

From a purely materialist standpoint, a void (note the small v) is generally understood to mean a region of space with a lower density of matter than is typical in the universe as a whole. These phenomena may have resulted from fluctuations of nascent energy in the early universe. Among the webs and filaments in which matter is distributed, the voids are the empty spaces between. Another type of physical emptiness can be found at the smallest scale of existence. The average distance between the nucleus of a hydrogen atom and the orbital shell of its electron is more than 10^{24} times the size of the smallest measurable distance. What is it that occupies this space? It is truly *Nothing*. Emptiness is thus conceivable as a physical space, but at scales so minute or so massive that they are difficult for the human mind to conceive.

As interesting as these concepts are, neither are the most applicable for the purpose of magical practice. *A* void is not *The* Void but learning to know and contemplate the former is a step towards better understanding the latter. A more useful definition for the purpose at hand is found in the cosmogenic concept of the Void. In the mythic and religious cosmology of many cultures, the Void is the nothingness that existed before all else. All that has ever or will ever exist emerged from it. It is primordial, predating thought and intent. Whether believed to be stirred or manipulated by a godform from some other, external place, or whether it was the nature of the Void itself to coalesce into creation, it is the progenitrix of all things.

Also of value from an esoteric standpoint is the Void as a metaphysical state. This is the emptiness known as *Sunyata*. The attainment of this state is the ultimate goal of several Buddhist schools of thought. It represents the divestment of desire and suffering. A great deal of material has been passed down from the oral and written transmissions on how to train the mind towards this goal. Even within Buddhist practices, the conception of this state is complicated by the various schools and sects. Any kind of worthwhile treatment of this topic is far beyond the scope of this work, but I encourage at least a cursory investigation of it. A satisfying encapsulation of the duality of the simplicity and complexity of the matter can be found in the *Book of Five Rings* by Miymoto Musashi. He observes that "Of course the void is nothingness. By knowing things that exist, you can know that which does not exist. That is the void."

In literature and popular media, the Void is often characterized as being hungry. In my experience this is not accurate. Humankind seems to have an unfortunate predilection for assigning sentient intent, and even malice to natural phenomenon that are considered dangerous or beyond our control or awareness. In short, we often fear that which we do not understand. Incidentally, this is also the process by which natural phenomena become personified as gods. But the Void in and of itself is utterly without sentience or intent for good or evil. It does not yearn, and it does not hunger. It is uncorrupted by any human emotion or modality. As such, it can be a potent magical construct to work with.

Apart from the countenance of its entirety, there is also disagreement in literature and among occultists on whether the Void is utterly empty, or rather is populated by entities outside of human experience. Although the distinction is my own, I tend to qualify the former as the *Primal* Void in my own studies in order to distinguish the two conceptualizations from one-another. These opposing viewpoints can each be used for various purposes, depending on the nature of the working being performed.

The first section of this book consists of a survey of the various esoteric and exoteric definitions and portrayals of the Void as a concept. This will serve as a foundation for the second section, which concerns the development of magical techniques which utilize the Void or its emanations in some way.

Caveats

There are dangers inherent with doing Void work, which must be acknowledged before beginning. Obsession, lethargy, and allowing too great of a degree of dissolution of the ego are only a few examples. Ongoing engagement with the Void can lead to a growing affinity for it. The "call of the void" is even a commonly known psychological phenomenon referring to the desire to perform self destructive acts, such as jumping from an obviously unsurvivable height. It is these moments that test our resilience in the face of oblivion. Existence is not easy, and there may always be a call to abandon it, however faint. Awareness of this fact allows for the construction of defenses against it.

The goal of Voidworking is to become an effective conduit for the power of the Void, not to seek a premature end of the Self.

Another concern is the psychic, physical, mental, and emotional toll that prolonged workings and the evocation of Void entities and energies can cause if proper precautions are not taken beforehand to mitigate these effects. Whether these repercussions are actually due to some external agent, or whether they originate within oneself based on a personal assumption of the capabilities of such entities, the resulting detriment to the well-being of the self can be just as real.

There are a number of methods that can be used to counteract the drain. These can be valuable when engaging in any type of magical practice, not just the ones described in this work. Some of these are merely common sense. You should never perform magical work when overly stressed, exhausted, or excessively impaired by the effects of consuming any substance. You should have a functional awareness and control of your mental state before beginning. It can also be useful to keep a journal of workings, along with their results, as well as any physical, mental, or emotional side effects that they might have upon you. Monitor yourself, or have someone you trust keep an eye on you for wild variations in behavior after any particular working. Practice some type of grounding technique. It can help dispel any residual psychic or mental funk that you may accumulate.

Willpower is a depletable, yet renewable resource, much like the way that water from a spring replenishes a well. If you consume it at a faster rate than it is refilled, you will find yourself scraping the bottom of your metaphorical well in order to get what you require. You should pace yourself in your works until you learn how fast your own personal supply is replenished. Sometimes it is necessary to set aside active magical practice for a time. Engage in hobbies or activities that are not as taxing, and allow yourself to recharge. Do research on your current paradigm, or on others that interest you. You might also be able to bolster yourself by drawing on the psychic energy of others, either consensually or not as you see fit. If you do engage in the latter, be aware that this in itself may cause lasting repercussions. No one appreciates a leech. Ultimately, if you experience difficulties that you cannot effectively manage on your own, seek assistance.

I feel safe asserting that the prevailing view in the contemporary western world is that engaging in the practice of magic is not a 'normal' thing for a person to do. That does not mean that it is unwise or unsafe, merely that it is outside of the mundane parameters of reality that we are socialized to accept. As such, you can likely expect reactions ranging from disapproval and disbelief at best, to scorn, derision, disgust, or physical endangerment at worst from those who come to find out what you are up to. How you choose to deal with this possibility is up to you, but be prepared to do so in some manner.

Magic is not irrational, but a dogmatic and unquestioning belief in any system or schema can be. Magic is a largely subjective practice, and sometimes one must agree to disagree with consensus reality, while still acknowledging the physical reality that underlies it, at least to the extent that our senses can perceive it. You still have to operate, at least to some degree, in the mundane world constructed largely by those who may be antithetical to your beliefs and practices. I've long remarked that even an Illuminated Adept has to pay the mortgage, and the Master of the Temple probably has to pump their own gasoline.

There is no right or wrong way to practice magic, in terms of keeping your work secret or revealing it and yourself as a magician. Let your circumstances and your best judgement inform your decision, with the understanding that once you are out and open, there is likely no going back. How much of a danger this may be to you can depend on many factors, and you should weigh them all. Even now in the 21st century, it can be a death sentence in some parts of the world.

A number of the techniques described in this work assume that you already have a functional understanding of the basic principles of magical and ritual working. If you lack this experience, you may still find value in the material, but I encourage you to first engage in a more general course of study and practice of Chaos Magic, traditional sorcery, or a Hermetic tradition of your choice. This will provide you with a solid foundation that can be enriched by this material rather than using this work as a starting point for your practice.

There is no shame in being a neophyte. Everyone who works magic has to start somewhere, and then deepen and broaden their practice over time. It can take many years of study to understand and master even a narrow swath of techniques. No one becomes an adept overnight. Practicing magic requires a strong will, which can in turn project as a big ego. Although a measure of self-worth and self-importance is certainly required, it need not be overwhelming. My advice is to attempt to maintain a sense of humility and wonder as you grow your skill set, and to ignore smirking know-it-alls and bitter cynics when they cross your path. It can be good to collaborate with others of like mind and purpose, but beware of those who would drain your energy and effort without providing a benefit to you.

There are no hard and fast rules regarding the actual practicing techniques of magical working. There are myriad traditions, sets of beings with which to work, and collections of spells from all around the world, over a span of millenia. The assertion that all of these can achieve desired results seems to indicate that there is an underlying mechanism behind them by which the actual work is done. They are all merely different interfaces that human beings have put upon them. Every bit of importance and gravitas bestowed upon the traditional tools and methods of each magical paradigm was created, practiced, and disseminated with intent by human action. The system that I am about to lay out for you is my own creation, but even so, it draws on many older sources and many disciplines, as all modern systems do.

It takes a combination of courage, curiosity, and vulnerability to engage with the Void.
Similarly, in order to practice magic to best effect, one must learn to maintain a balance between that openness and a finely-tuned variety of egotism. The Void is an *awesome* concept, in the original meaning of the word. With all of this in mind, let us press onward.

I: Laying the Foundation

Religion and Cosmology

The concept of a primordial void state from which the universe emerges is present in the creation myths of many early cultures. In some, it is conceived as a boundless emptiness, devoid of matter or structure. In others, this void is envisioned as a vast body of water. In either case, it is from this *ur*-state that order emerges, either as a self-organizational process, or with direction from the earliest gods of a people. Following are some examples that illustrate the similarities between these myths:

Then was not non-existent nor existent: there was no realm of air, no sky beyond it.
What covered in, and where? and what gave shelter? Was water there, unfathomed depth of water? Death was not then, nor was there aught immortal: no sign was there, the day's and night's divider. That One Thing, breathless, breathed by its own nature: apart from it was nothing whatsoever. Darkness there was: at first concealed in darkness this All was indiscriminated chaos. All that existed then was void and formless: by the great power of Warmth was born that Unit. Thereafter rose Desire in the beginning, Desire, the primal seed and germ of Spirit. Sages who searched with their heart's thought discovered the existent's kinship in the non-existent.

- Rig Veda, Mandala 10, Hymn CXXIX: Hymn of Creation. Circa 1200 BCE

This is one of the cases that implies that a great expanse of water predated the existence of the world, and that an order began to emerge from this state without the guidance of a god.

In the beginning God created the heaven and the earth. And the earth was without form, and void; and darkness was upon the face of the deep. And the Spirit of God moved upon the face of the waters. And God said, Let there be light: and there was light. And God saw the light, that it was good: and God divided the light from the darkness.

- The Bible, King James, Book 1: Genesis, Circa 6th century BCE

This is likely the most widely-known creation myth in the western world. The god of Abraham pre-dated the Void, and brought it forth as a precursor to the rest of creation.

Verily at the first Chaos (Χαοσ) came to be, but next wide-bosomed Earth, the ever-sure foundations of all the deathless ones who hold the peaks of snowy Olympus, and dim Tartarus in the depth of the wide-pathed Earth, and Eros (Love), fairest among the deathless gods, who unnerves the limbs and overcomes the mind and wise counsels of all gods and all men within them. From Chaos came forth Erebus and black Night; but of Night were born Aether and Day, whom she conceived and bare from union in love with Erebus.

- Hesiod, The Theogony, Circa 700 BCE

In this myth, the formless void coalesced into an egg, and from this were born Gaea, Tarterus, Eros, Erebus, and Nyx, the primordial sentient beings that gave structure to the universe and spawned the Titans.

In earliest times did Ymir live: was not sea nor land nor salty waves, neither earth was there nor upper heaven but a gaping nothing and green things nowhere.

- The Voluspa (The Prophecy of the Seeress), from the Poetic Edda, Circa 1270 CE

The gaping nothing that the Seeress referred to was known as the *Ginnungagap* in Old Norse. This term derives ultimately from the Proto-Indo-European *ghan-*, meaning to yawn. The myths also state that the cosmos will be plunged back into the Void at the time of *Ragnarok*, the twilight of the gods. After the wolves Skoll and Hati devour the Sun and the Moon, the stars shall go out, leaving only a great darkness, and the land sinks below the sea. But this is not the end. The Seeress also foretold that the world would emerge again from the still waters. This act was not done by any of the gods, but rather implied to be self-instantiated.

Non-existence is named the Antecedent of heaven and earth; and Existence is named the Mother of all things. In eternal non-existence, therefore, man seeks to pierce the primordial mystery; and, in eternal existence, to behold the issues of the Universe. But these two are one and the same, and differ only in name. This sameness (or existence and non-existence) I call the abyss — the abyss of abysses — the gate of all mystery.

- The Dao De Jing, attributed to the sixth-century BCE Chinese sage Lao Tzu.

This story addresses the differentiation of that which is from that which was before, and asserts the difference to be illusory. This perspective seems to answer the question of whether or not the previous state of unity still exists in a state beyond time and creation. Until one acknowledges that there is no difference between these epochs, true understanding of neither is possible. This is also the mystery alluded to in the Rig Veda.

Parallel to all of these myths is the theory of the Big Bang, the most widely accepted secular cosmological model to describe the creation of the Universe. In this model, it is assumed that all existence can be traced back to a single point of infinite density that exploded and rapidly expanded approximately 13.8 billion years ago. Any concept of the nascent universe expanding *into* some space is absent, as space itself is the medium of expansion. Physics cannot answer the question of what was here before there was a "here".

An alternate theory suggests that rather than from a singularity, matter and energy emerged from fluctuations in the vacuum energy present in the fabric of space itself. This is strongly analogous to several of the mythological origin stories. This concept of emergence is one that is frequently applied to describe the appearance of life, and of the possibility of the development of a true artificial intelligence. In complex systems, unexpected and occasionally unexplainable behaviors *emerge* from constituent subsystems. What appears to be empty space is actually a roiling chaotic sea of quantum foam.

Fluctuations at this scale can propagate upward and produce persistent artifacts of matter and energy. Just as virtual particles are constantly created and destroyed in the physical world, potentialities are likewise continually emerging and being subsumed by the metaphysical Void. It is not a stable or placid construct.

Even the vacuum empty space itself is not the most devoid physical construct that is theorized to exist. There are mathematical conjectures in certain string theory models that describe bubbles of nothingness, not even the spacial substrate itself, that could form in our universe and essentially consume it.

The most important idea in terms of magical practice to take away from these myths and theories is the concept of creating something from nothing, or *creatio ex nihilo* as it is known in Latin. The act of instantiating matter out of "thin air" so to speak. In the phenomenal world, this is obviously beyond the capability of magic to produce directly, but in the imaginal world of visualization, all things are possible. This is contrasted against the creation of organized existence from a prior state, or *creatio ex materia*.
Even in these scenarios, the Void may play a role, as in the case of the Golden Egg in Vedic belief. This was thought to have floated in a state of non-existence prior to fragmenting into the material worlds. It is thought that nothing preceded it. Indeed, *Nothing* did precede it.

Depending on your view on the nature of the Void, either as a *thing* or as *not a thing*, either of these paradigms may apply to your use in magical applications. This may seem like a cop-out, but the myths that have been passed down to the present day through countless generations, based on oral traditions rich in metaphor, may have been misconstrued and mistranslated by much later scribes and archivists. This has resulted in a potentially false dichotomy. Even within the same sources there are contradictions. In the previously mentioned *Hymn of Creation*, it is written both that at first "even nothingness was not" and "At first there was only darkness wrapped in darkness. All this was only unillumined cosmic water." Here as in other sources such as the Babylonian *Enuma Elish*, water and non-existence seem to be interchangeable. As confusing as this may seem, it is all in accord with a working magical approach to the Void. Revel in the seemingly conflicting nature of these differing perspectives, and let their contemplation be a source of meditational inspiration.

Earliest man, when attempting to understand his world and to define the source of all that is, would have looked to the sea and the sky as the most vast and mysterious of concepts that he had encountered. It is only natural that creation would be couched in these terms, but writ large. Ironically, the conflation of primordial emptiness and the boundless waters is correct in the sense that life on Earth began in the water and then emerged onto land. Even if all of creation did not emerge from the depths, we did.

If the state of primogenial non-existence transcends the physical universe, then so must it be outside the bounds and limitations of time. Thus this state is as conceptually available in any era as it was at the smallest possible measurement of time after existence was spawned. In certain models of reality, one can access any point in the timeline of a dimension one degree lower than one's own. In this vein, a sorcerer can transcend their own epoch and access the power of the state of unlimited potential. It is not in veneration but rather in imitation of the gods that acts of Voidworking are performed. It is from the paradoxical state of nothing and not-nothing from which magic roils forth, wrought and guided by the Will of the worker.

Philosophy

Some of the earliest roots in Western philosophy involve different schools of thought arguing over whether or not the Void existed, and what the implications of this opinion were for creation, movement, and change in the world. In the sixth century B.C.E., Anaximander of Miletus was the progenitor of the concept of the *Apeiron,* or the boundless, a prospective source of existence, as it was preceded by nothing. It was eternal and unborn. From this original state, a shard or germ was thought to have differentiated itself, and subsequently formed the firmament and the earth. In contrast, Anaximander's contemporary Parmenides of Elea and his followers held that the world was eternal, and had not come from nothing, and that movement was an illusion. Two centuries later, the school of Democritus of Abdera believed that matter originated from the accretion of infinitesimal *atoms* seething in the substrate of Chaos.

One of the ways in which the concept of the Void in its guise as the abyss is most commonly encountered is in the works of Friedrich Nietzsche. He warned in *Beyond Good and Evil* that "...if thou gaze long into an abyss, the abyss will also gaze into thee."

Although this point of view embodies an envisioning of the Void as an archetypically negative phenomenon, a so-called "evil dwells in darkness" schema, there is still value in this assertion. It can be interpreted as a warning against engaging in the excessive practice of existential nihilism. This perspective, which posits that existence is devoid of intrinsic meaning, is not a prerequisite for Voidworking, but the concepts could be thought of as close cousins. Immersion in one of these practices might well lead to indulging in the other.

It is tempting to conflate a guiding life principle that embraces nothingness itself with a path of magical practice which centers on nothingness, but whereas the former can be thought of as an operational meta-framework, the latter is more restricted in scope, at least initially. Since the annihilation of the self is an inevitable fate for all in due time, there is certainly merit in gaining an understanding of this ultimate destination of life's journey, but this awareness does not necessitate the abandonment of ethics, aesthetics, or morality.

If the despair of knowing that one is bound for oblivion becomes overwhelming, then an injection of pure fatalism can serve as a balm. Assume the position that your fate was

Voidworking

determined before you drew your first breath, and laugh at the adversity of the absurd world into which you were born. The act of *screaming into the void* is a popular trope that summarizes the frustration and terror that result from the realization of one's circumstances. Besides being a means of catharsis, this can be reframed as a positive and creative act. The simple act of asserting your own existence, albeit brief as it will be in a cosmic scale, is a foundational operation. Workers of Will must dance on the knife's edge of extreme egotism and the death of that self-same ego. This in turn reveals the fact that ego itself is just another tool.

An effective approach to living is to navigate life within an optimistic, existentialist framework, accepting the consequences for your actions while realizing that you are one player in a cast of billions. Understand that bad things happen to good people, and vice-versa, and that the world is an arbitrary and patently unfair place. Once you are armed with this information, determine how you wish to comport yourself, and do so, however consensus reality may try to constrain you.

One should discard preconceptions that assume the state of nothingness to be tainted in some way. Miyamoto Musashi writes that "In the void is virtue, and no evil." Besides the reference to the state of no-mind, which I will address later, I also propose that he may be implying that this state is unsullied by human intent that could only serve to taint it. In this regard, the Void serves only as a mirror to the self. Any malevolent intent to be found within it is projected by mankind itself. If you carry no such intentions into the Void with you, then you will find none there to vex you. On the other hand, if you are shrouded in a cloak of excessive ego, you will find yourself laid bare, as such brittle conceits are sublimated in its ineffable vastness.

Contemporary Magic

A number of modern magicians have worked in various ways with their own conceptions of the Void. I encourage the study of multiple sources to gain a broader understanding of all of their points of view. Following is a review of several of the sources that I have found to be most salient.

Aleister Crowley, one of the most widely known occultists of the 20th century, describes his conception of the abyss thusly:

The name of the Dweller in the Abyss is Choronzon, but he is not really an individual. The Abyss is empty of being; it is filled with all possible forms, each equally inane, each therefore evil in the only true sense of the word – that is, meaningless but malignant, in so far as it craves to become real. These forms swirl senselessly into haphazard heaps like <u>dust devils</u>, and each such chance aggregation asserts itself to be an individual and shrieks, "I am I!" though aware all the time that its elements have no true bond; so that the slightest disturbance dissipates the delusion just as a horseman, meeting a dust devil, brings it in showers of sand to the earth.

- The Confessions of Aleister Crowley

The definition brings to mind the *Theory of Forms*, described among Plato's various dialogues, that there is some imaginal place or state which contains the ideal forms of all objects conceivable. When an artisan creates an object, the application of this concept is brought to bear. The mind of the creator conceives an image of that which is to be created. This is the form, which is brought into physical existence through the skill and experience of the maker. In this way, they become the interface between the place of all forms and the physical world. A magician performs a similar act, but rather than an artifact, the work being created is a world state in which the desired effect is manifest. It is designed via intense visualization. I'll discuss the practical application of this technique later.

Despite this parallel, Crowley did not view the abyss as a source of useful manifestations, but as a gulf that had to be crossed in order to achieve one's maximum potential as a magician. Choronzon, the Demon of Dispersions, composed of pure negation, must be bested in a contest of wills in order to achieve this crossing. Crowley believed that he achieved this goal during a magical working performed with his disciple Victor Neuberg in Algiers in 1909.

The demon that stands in the way of self-actualization is itself an appropriation from the monomyth, or Hero's Journey described by Joseph Campbell. The hero must face the powerful father figure, and allow his own ego to be shattered in the process, so that he may re-emerge in a reconstituted and wiser state than when he entered the ordeal. The soul and psyche of the hero undergo a truly alchemical transformation, akin to smelting the pure metal from raw ore. The trauma of this passage is commensurate with the hero's desire to cling to their existing structures and preconceptions. As Grant Morrison wrote in *Pop Magic!*, "The personality on the brink of the Abyss will do anything, say anything, and find any excuse to avoid taking this disintegrating step into non-being."

The power and ferocity of the guardian of the Abyss, and the difficulty of passing its trials does not depend on the Void itself, but is rather determined by the magician. Each person has a different conception of the opposition that lies between them and the ultimate goal of greatest self-actualization. Some may require a prolonged campaign that lasts for years. Others may undergo the metaphysical equivalent of sitting down to have a beer with their demon, then bid it adieu and pass nonchalantly into satori. How this process unfolds depends largely on the mindset and degree of preparation and conditioning the magician undergoes prior to attempting to best this foe. As I stated before, the only malice to be found in the Void is that which is brought in. One aspect of success in this contest, however it is accomplished, is the realization that the Abyss is not a thing to be crossed or conquered as much as it's nature is to be understood.

In *Liber Null*, Seminal Chaos Magician Peter Carroll advises prospective adepts to "Reside in the Void, Be Vacuous, Have No Mind." By this practice, he asserts that one can achieve the state of "constant magical consciousness." He suggests using a "visualized shape" to assist with annulling thought for the purpose of entering the Void "as completely as possible", and then dissolving this shape itself, leaving consciousness in the vacuous state. Carroll also makes reference to Choronzon in *Psychonaut*:

We also have a regrettable capacity to become obsessed with the mere products of our genius, mistaking them for the genius itself. These obsessional side effects have a genetic name, Choronzon, or perhaps the demons Choronzon, for its name is multiple. To worship these creations is to imprison oneself in madness and to invoke eventual disaster.

He advises that Choronzon be banished whenever it manifests.

The modern magician known as Thomas Chaote has a more pragmatic and sanguine approach to the Void as a source of inspiration and magical power. In *Void Magick*, he writes:

Confronting with and getting used to this idea of nothingness, discovering it inside the self in one lifetime, making peace with a possibility of returning to a bleak destination, connecting and directing Void energies holds multiple benefits and is part of a different path of spiritual enlightenment. In rivers of experienced hollowness lies a final conclusion and thus escape... Void holds and radiates with greater power and possible dominion over the world of defined thought and its forms.

Chaote addresses the concepts of disintegration and nullification, in both offensive and defensive magical workings, as well as illusion and enchantment applications of void influence and energy.

All of these sources can provide inspiration towards a greater understanding of the perils and possibilities of this type of magical work. Whether you use their techniques verbatim, or deconstruct them into components for rework into your own system, you should be inspired, but not constrained, by the offerings of those who have traversed this path before you.

Popular Culture

In his *Exegesis*, Philip K. Dick observed that the divine manifests in the lowest strata of existence. It hides in the trash in an alley and the detritus in the gutter. I've observed that useful magical concepts often do the same. The Void is a frequent fixture in literary works of fantasy and horror, as well as in video games, music, and film. It is unwise to assume that the common nature of these sources renders them any less valid than any traditional scripture or myth. In the eyes of a canny sorcerer, all of these fictions are equally valid and ripe for appropriation and incorporation into a syncretic personal magical paradigm. As in Shamatha meditation, no thought is any more or less valid than any other.

Fiction

In his novel *Imajica*, Clive Barker conceived of a place known as the *In Ovo*. This is the wasteland void that separates the earth, or The Fifth Dominion, from the other four Dominions. It must be traversed, and its lethal inhabitants avoided in order to pass between our world and the others. By nature, it is akin to Crowley's concept of the abyss:

In between the Reconciled Dominions and the Fifth is a state called the In Ovo. It's an ether, in which things that have ventured from their worlds are imprisoned.
...the inhabitants of the In Ovo beggared the bizarreness of any ocean floor. They had forms and appetites that no book had ever set down. They had rages and frustrations that were centuries old.

In the mythos of the book, a Maestro of sufficient power can also summon the various beings that are adrift in this space into our world to do their bidding as lovers, servants or assassins. These amount to the same forms that Crowley described, but instead of ignoring these proto-entities, their patterns are made flesh in our Dominion by the Maestro.

The works of H.P. Lovecraft approach the Void from the stance of cosmic horror. To open his best-known short story, *The Call of Cthulhu*, he writes:

The most merciful thing in the world, I think, is the inability of the human mind to correlate all its contents. We live on a placid island of ignorance in the midst of black seas of infinity, and it was not meant that we should voyage far.

Lovecraft's mythos are chiefly concerned with the

machinations of a pantheon of terrible beings of various factions that primarily exist outside the space-time of our universe. A passage in the famed, fictional grimoire *The Necronomicon* states that "The Old Ones were, the Old Ones are, and the Old Ones shall be. Not in the spaces we know, but between them." Not all of these beings are malevolent, but even to those that are not, mankind is thought to be utterly insignificant. To behold most of these entities is to be stricken utterly mad. Regardless of this, in the works of Lovecraft, his collaborators, and successors, many of these beings have cults that revere them and work to further their ends in the world.

Lovecraft speaks directly on the idea of ego dissolution, and his horror regarding this possibility in his story *Through the Gates of the Silver Key*:

Merging with nothingness is peaceful oblivion; but to be aware of existence and yet to know that one is no longer a definite being distinguished from other beings - that one no longer has a self - that is the nameless summit of agony and dread.

Many of Lovecraft's stories are cautionary tales that describe the cost and consequences of mankind trying to look beyond the veil of ignorance that is our cosmic mercy. In the tale above, Randolph Carter passes through gates to the outer reaches of the universe and beyond, where the power and depth of the secrets revealed to him is matched only by the terror he experiences.

Ironically, the description of one of Lovecraft's entities,

Voidworking

Yog-Sothoth, is reminiscent of the Dao: "Yog-Sothoth is the gate. Yog-Sothoth is the key and guardian of the gate. Past, present, future, all are one in Yog-Sothoth." This being, which is physically comprised of a collection of luminous spheres, exists beyond concepts of space and time:

It was an All-in-One and One-in-All of limitless being and self — not merely a thing of one Space-Time continuum, but allied to the ultimate animating essence of existence's whole unbounded sweep — the last, utter sweep which has no confines and which outreaches fancy and mathematics alike. It was perhaps that which certain secret cults of earth have whispered of as Yog-Sothoth, and which has been a deity under other names

Outside of the literature, there is even a current of Chaos Magic that uses many of these beings as their godforms of choice. Detailed material on how to petition these entities, while outside the scope of this work, should be easy to procure. Like the Void itself, Lovecraft's work is experiencing a surge in popularity in the early 21st century, possibly due to the elevated level of global anxiety and uncertainty.

In *The Hyperion Cantos* book series by Dan Simmons, the *Void Which Binds* is the term given to the dimension that contains human consciousness manifest as waveforms, and through which superluminal communication and transportation are possible via advanced technology.

Music

It's fitting that such a compelling, disturbing, and powerful subject as the Void has served as inspiration for musicians. It may be as the psychological sense of losing oneself in the Void, as represented by the Nine Inch Nails or Kiss songs *Into The Void*, or as the vastness of space in the Black Sabbath song of the same name. Die Krupps allude to the arcane aspect of the Void in their song *The Gods of Void*. In it, deceivers are compared to demons that must be exorcised and banished. One of my favorite references is in the System of a Down song *Aerials*:

Life is a waterfall
We're one in the river
And one again after the fall
Swimming through the void
We hear the word
We lose ourselves
But we find it all?

This evokes both the fluid nature of the Void, as well as the Gnostic/Hermetic premise that we are all merely aspects of a larger whole entity.

There are literally hundreds of songs that reference the Void in one of its various aspects, and it would be absurd to try and catalog them all here. If desired, a playlist of appropriate songs can be assembled in order to serve as a priming mechanism prior to engaging in Voidworking. Their lyrics may also serve as inspiration for the construction of incantations.

Video Games

The Void is also a concept found in a number of video games such as Destiny, Dragon Age, Dishonored, World of Warcraft, and many others. It is often assumed to be the source of dark or shadow power, whether psychic or magical, and can be seen as either sentient or not. The power that emanates from the Void can be channeled into our world as weapons, armor, or servitor entities. It is from these unlikely sources that the modern mythology of the Void is being constructed. Since the Void is an imaginal space, it is only fitting to be explored in these virtual worlds. These conceptualizations can be used as the basis for one's own magical workings. It's generally easier to co-opt an idea than to generate one, although there is a great deal of satisfaction to be had as the result of designing personal magical constructs.

One particularly useful conceit from the Dishonored franchise is the personification of the Void in the form of the Outsider. This offers an alternative to trying to relate to an abstraction for workings that might benefit from the more approachable interface of a being that may be conversed with. The Outsider was created by a cult who wished to more effectively understand the nature of the Void. There is a note in this game that beautifully captures the essence of the difficulty of this understanding:

We lack the language to express the Void in all its complexities. We have no words for its beauty. There is the rich, velvety darkness of the depths of the ocean. The hollow hues of the sky on

a starless night. The cold color when you close your eyes to moonlight. The mottled pigments of a bruise on tender skin. The sharp black at the corners of your vision as you faint from exhaustion. A crumbled anointment of old blood.
Your own face reflected faintly in dark glass.

In the virtual reality game *Boneworks*, the Void is conceived as another dimension, outside of time and space, which is comprised of vast unstable energy. This "void energy" is used as the power source for the in-universe virtual world. In an almost Gnostic approach to breaking out of the illusory world, the possibility is raised that humans can shed their perceived physical form and pass into the Void as a sentient, disembodied consciousness. It is also implied that humans in such a state could also incarnate back into any desired form that exists in the physical world.

Film

The 2016 horror film *The Void* references the concept in a Lovecraftian sense, as the protagonists find themselves trapped in a hospital which contains a gateway to cosmic horror. A number of Lovecraft's own works have also been adapted to film, and these all to a greater or lesser extent reflect his own views on the terror of the far-flung reaches of space and mind. A strong homage to his work is found in the film *In the Mouth of Madness*, in which the nameless horrors intrude into our own world, empowered by the belief of readers who are unaware that the stories they have been consuming were not mere fiction. Again, in these various works, the Void is viewed in a negative aspect of fear and ignorance. Unsurprisingly, there is little love to be found in the inscrutable.

Hopefully this examination of the aspects of the Void in various disciplines of human endeavor has provided a suitable foundation upon which to start creating a personal magical system that will take advantage of this rich set of concepts. Whether as an internal or external symbol set, the sublime power and purity of the primordial state of pre-existence and emptiness is available to those who choose to embrace it. The Void is not hungry, nor evil. It is not sentient, but within it lies the ultimate potential for both creation and destruction. Its vastness and depth are beyond the scope of human comprehension, but through allegory and symbolism it can be understood and manipulated. Too, a greater sense of comfort with these ideas can be gained through exposure via these more familiar avenues. Magic is empowered by acceptance and structure, and can be thwarted by the lack of either.

Part II: Voidworking

Despite myriad theories, including my own ideas which were described in *Quantum Sorcery*, the exact mechanism by which imaginal intent results in the desired corresponding changes in physical reality remains a mystery. Fortunately, we who practice magic don't need to solve this mystery in order to make it effective, even if we care to know. We learn to focus our intent by whichever methods speak most deeply to us, and we get results. Perhaps there is some receptor capability within the Universe itself that is listening for instructions, and our lot is to hijack this capability for our own ends. What matters is that something *can* be made from nothing, and despite Nietzsche's protestation, that order *can* be made from disorder.

All of the information and concepts pertaining to the Void that I have investigated throughout this book have been leading toward the specific goal of utilizing the Void as a conceit in magical workings. Whether as a philosophical anchor, a source of visualization, or as a perceived wellspring from which forms and power may be coaxed forth, the Void can be a very useful symbol for empowering acts of sorcery.

Drawing upon both esoteric and exoteric conceptions of the Void, the paradigm of Voidworking promotes the practice of dissolution of aspects of the discrete Self for purposes of removing the illusion of separation between the sorcerer and the Universe. By the elimination of this perceived barrier, the "magical link" between the worker and the environment in which the magic is performed can be strengthened. This link is one of the core concepts in the practice of sorcery. As in the hero's journey, the ego can be deconstructed and then re-established according to a desired design rather than the messy, random, and crude construct that accretes naturally. Further, the Void itself is conceived as a source of energy that can be tapped for the purpose of enhancing the inherent power of the magical worker.

The question of whether this practice is black, white, or grey in nature is irrelevant. It is neither the exclusive purview of either the Right or Left Hand path. The Void transcends all such Manichaean dichotomies. It is also above and beyond the sphere of any deity of any faith. It is a universal, primordial concept, accessible to any and all. However, by most reckoning, Voidworking will be categorized as a Left Hand magical path. Under the definition proposed by Michael Aquino, it would certainly be, as it *involves the conscious attempt to preserve and strengthen one's isolate, psychocentric existence against the objective universe (OU) while apprehending, comprehending, and influencing a varying number of subjective universes (SU).* This system certainly does not seek to support the knowledge and conversation of one's Holy Guardian Angel. That said, there is no baleful intent in the techniques described herein in and of themselves. They can be used for constructive or destructive purposes as you see fit. The magician must own both the benefits and the consequences of their actions.

What is Magic?

Before proceeding to the description of specific magical techniques, I feel obligated to describe what I mean when I use the word *magic*, and how that is similar to and different from other definitions. Note that I generally do not use Crowley's stylized spelling of the word. I assume that if you're reading this, then you know well what is meant by the term without the addition of the "special k".

There are numerous opinions on how magic should be defined. In *Magick in Theory and Practice*, Aleister Crowley wrote that "Magick is the Science and Art of causing Change to occur in conformity with Will." He also stated that "ANY required change may be effected by the application of the proper kind and degree of Force in the proper manner, through the proper medium to the proper object." Although this definition is likely the best known among modern occultists, it is not necessarily the best one.

In *S.S.O.T.B.M.E.*, Ramsey Dukes wrote:

Magic is a technique by which the human mind attempts to operate upon its world. As such it is similar to Art, Religion and Science, but note that the term 'its world' is meant to embrace not only the physical universe but also all phenomena, objective or subjective, which do not respond to direct control.

It is from Duke's definition that I first began to examine the relationship between the mind and the universe that it inhabits, which informed my own beliefs regarding the

Voidworking

nature of magic that I described in *Quantum Sorcery*. I theorize that magic is the phenomenon of the direct fundamental interaction between the mind and the physical universe itself at the most fundamental level. This paradigm is also informed by the principle of the microcosm and macrocosm as described on the Emerald Tablet of Hermes Trismegistus: *What is above is like what is below. What is below is like what is above.* The model of desired reality is formed in the mind and encoded through various techniques into an instruction for the universe to instantiate. Everything else, all trappings, agents, and systems are useful frameworks to assist in facilitating this action.

Some seekers may believe that the true secrets of effective magic are held solely by any one of a number of initiatory magical organizations. Unfortunately, many of these groups are far more concerned with control than they are about fellowship or teaching useful magical practices to their members. Bombastic rituals are concocted, and demands are made of the aspirant that seek to break down critical thinking and emotional fortitude. Adherence to these directives is required in order to gain further knowledge of the group's vaunted secrets, and to advance in rank within the order.

These social power games are a useless distraction from personal advancement, and in some cases they are thinly veiled attempts by charismatic narcissists to gain control over as many underlings as possible. This is not to say that all magical groups or fraternities are without merit, only to be cautious in determining to whom you pledge your loyalty and devote the energy of your workings. If someone is demanding your absolute and unquestioning devotion, or telling you that theirs is the only true and correct method to achieve the results that you are looking for, then I suggest that you should keep one hand on your wallet and one eye on the exit. Be wary, keep your critical faculties fully engaged, and determine early on just how far you are willing to follow someone else's program before you sever your ties.

Although care must be taken when performing magical works with others, there is much to be gained by working with those of like mind and purpose. If such a cohort can be assembled, treat it as any group of co-workers. Maintain an atmosphere of mutual respect. If this cannot be achieved, then you are working with the wrong people. It is only natural that one or a few members of such a group will tend towards roles of leadership and guidance, but any pledges or oaths made among such a group should be aimed towards mutual devotion and support, not a band of sycophants propping up the ego of a figurehead. Work together only as long as it is beneficial to do so. If a group becomes irredeemably dysfunctional, then it should be dissolved with as little rancor as possible.

There is no great secret to performing magic. Any sentient being capable of expressing a conscious desire, and capable of learning the appropriate techniques to manifest that desire can do it. It's not in the blood, and it's not a spiritual gift. It's in the mind of the magus so to speak. There are many traditions and frameworks that can be used for magical work, from the simple to the elaborate, and from the ancient to the modern. Any or all of these systems may be effective, if the user believes that they work.

Why is this so? The reason is that all magical systems are subjective. Whatever mechanism that magical practice activates within the physical universe is the same, regardless of how it is accessed. Whether spiritualists, materialists, or perhaps both camps are actually correct in their suppositions of what this force or phenomenon is, and what its ultimate source may be is irrelevant. There is no one true way. Magic has the power that you give it, whether you believe that this power originates within yourself, or whether you are merely a conduit. You are the architect and the builder. If you do not believe in the efficacy of your magic, with all of the Will you can muster, then there is little chance that it will be effective.

Some practitioners seem to delight in the exaltation of so-called High Magic, while denigrating Low Magic. In a similar vein, practitioners of the Right and Left hand paths spar across subjective boundaries. Don't waste your time in this needless churn. Through experimentation you will find the techniques that work for you. Assemble your system from these and ignore irrelevant labels. Your undertaking is nothing less than the reimagining of reality itself

Why Do Magic?

Now that a working definition of magic has been established, the question naturally arises: Why would someone want to do it in the first place? A short, flippant answer that I once gave to this question is "What else would I do?" More seriously, there may be a number of reasons to undertake the practice. In my experience, the foremost of these is often the desire for power or control, either over oneself and one's own circumstances, or over others via the subversion of their will by the magician. In some cases, it is a personal crisis that first causes someone to look for a solution that is outside the bounds of their normal capabilities. For some this results in the pursuit of religion. Again, for some, that may be a viable alternative, but it comes with a great deal of constraint. Another reason to take up magic may be the result of simple human curiosity. Some people simply have to dive down a rabbit hole when they stumble across one. Study leads to practice.

Practicing magic is different than embracing a religious dogma. Through magic, we seek to write our own truths and define our own path. We do not subscribe to the idea that there is a deity with a grand plan, pre-scripted and determined, in which we are consigned to play some small role. This is not to imply that working with godforms is anathema, but don't bend the knee or bow your head to them without question. Too, we reject the concept that our life trajectory is predetermined. Magic is the antithesis of fatalism. This is where my own bias exerts an influence on my approach. For purposes of my practice, I assume that the universe is non-deterministic, and that at least local free-will is possible. There are magical systems that originate within a deterministic framework, but I do not work in them. If the universe truly is fully deterministic, then I really don't have a choice in the matter anyway, but where is the fun in that?

This approach is not without drawbacks. Even as we can claim credit for our own successes, we must also bear the blame for our own failures and shortcomings. For this reason, prolonged magical practice nearly inevitably results in the desire to become more effective and efficient at the simple art of living through skillful means. Those who are content to blunder through life without awareness or accountability are not well-suited to the rigors of self-improvement and reflection that are the hallmark of a seasoned sorcerer.

In my own experience, I first took up divination magic during adolescence out of a desire to better my circumstances by gathering deeper and broader information about the world, and how I fit into it. I did not want control over anyone other than myself, but I did very much want that. For a number of years, I did subscribe to a procession of religious faiths, most of which also included the practice of various forms of ritual and magical practices. Ultimately, I came to the conclusion that a non-theistic form of magic suited me better. Thus I began to synthesize my own systems from all of the various forms that I had been exposed to. I believe that mine may be a common pattern of development among magical practitioners.

Magic can be used as a weapon or a shield, to gain guidance, or to procure an agent to act on your behalf. It can give you the capability to influence the thoughts or actions of others. It is a means to an end, not an end in and of itself. It is a skill to apply when mundane methods fail to achieve desired results. Some magicians will work spells or perform rituals for trivial reasons. To each their own, but I discourage this practice. The reason for doing a working need not be earth-shattering, but it should be specific. Magic is an act of focus and Will. If there is no reason for doing it, how can these be applied to it? Gaining experience and proficiency through the repetition and refinement of one's art certainly a valid reason if no greater purpose is at hand, but even this should be done with some kind of plan in mind.

Like the Void itself, magic is without inherent morality. It is the ethics of the practitioner that dictate the disposition of the work. If one chooses to inhibit the will of, or bring harm to another, that is on the magician. Various systems have the assumption of a law of feedback, such as the Three-fold Law in which some Wiccans believe. The general concept of these is that what goes around comes around, and if you perpetrate acts of evil, then the Universe will return this intent upon you. Some have also referred to this as Karma, but that is an oversimplification and gross misunderstanding of that concept. Other systems, such as LaVey's Satanism reject the idea of a feedback effect.

My own approach is simple. It can best be summed up as "Don't be more of an asshole than you have to be." In general, I do not seek to subvert the Will of others without their consent, and I prefer a reactive defensive posture as opposed to aggression. This is a conscious choice, and each magician must decide for themselves how they will comport themselves. It is no one's prerogative to judge the choice of another in this regard. I have been known to issue a curse when necessary, but I more often bless those whose paths I cross with wishes of good health and good fortune. I have found that in general, like does seem to attract like in terms of action and attitude in the world. I seek to lessen the amount of suffering in the world, and so I choose to sow seeds of benevolence when I can. This is a conscious choice on my part. It is not fear of divine retribution that guides me.

Regardless of how you conduct yourself, some religions will condemn (some quite literally) any worker of Will whether or not they perform acts that are generally perceived to be evil or harmful or not. If a faith predisposes its followers to engage in such behavior, then it is an instant red flag that it, and likely its members, should be avoided if possible.

Tuning the Magical Mind

An essential part of doing magic is achieving a state of mind state in which we are convinced that our workings can have an actual effect. More precisely, the internal and external factors that inhibit successful application of the Will must be counteracted. For best results, it is essential to engage in some regimen of training and mental conditioning that will facilitate reaching the required mental space. As the Void is a thing that is not a thing, by contemplating this *no-thing* we can train our mind to emulate its state.

Dave Smith

In the Cula-Sunnata Sutta, The Lesser Discourse on Emptiness, it is stated that:

...a bhikkhu gives attention to the single state (of non-voidness) dependent on (the presence of) perception of the base consisting of infinite consciousness. His mind enters into the perception of the base consisting of infinite consciousness and acquires confidence, steadiness and decision.

And later:

'Whatever monks and divines in the future will enter upon and abide in a voidness that will be purified and unsurpassed by any other, they will all of them enter upon and abide in this voidness that is pure and unsurpassed by any other.

Greatly simplified, I take this to mean that in order to enter a clear state of mind, one must enter into a state of void consciousness, to put out of mind the concerns of earthly life. The distractions of the world are not present in the void state of mind, also known as *wuxin*. This practice is fundamental in Zen and Taoism. Nothingness itself is something, It is a thing that must be banished from the mind, and thus "the single state (of non-voidness)" is attained. This is a significant realization. When consciousness is freed of preconception, then absolute freedom to act becomes possible.

By achieving the state of "no-mind" and removing clutter and preconception, the mind can be trained to exhibit a paradoxical state of awareness, at once laser-focused and diffuse. As the samurai Itō Ittōsai wrote regarding the training of swordsmen: "Therefore it is essential that you remove all doubt from your technique. You must vigorously train yourself so that you are empty, the void." Musashi also espoused the state as key: "When your spirit is not in the least clouded, when the clouds of bewilderment clear away, there is the true void."

To clear the mind of matters extraneous to the task at hand is vital for the success of magical work. Austin Spare, the seminal Chaos Magician knew this principle well. He described it in *The Book of Pleasure*:

The primordial vacuity (or belief) is not by the exercise of focussing the mind on a
negation of all conceivable things, the identity of unity and duality, chaos and uniformity, etc., etc., but by doing it now, not eventually. Perceive, and feel without the necessity of an opposite, but by its relative.

Spare's mind state of *vacuity* is often referred to as *gnosis* by those who use his method of sigil creation. In my opinion, it is an unfortunate misappropriation of the term, and I tend to use his original nomenclature. Regardless of terminology, this mental tabula rasa is the starting point for all else. Unfortunately, there are several possible impediments that must be overcome in order to achieve this state. These can be loosely grouped into those that are external to the self and those that are internal.

In *The Phenomenon of Man*, French philosopher Pierre Teilhard de Chardin coined the idea of the *noosphere* as the collective sphere of human thought that surrounds us:

A glow ripples outward from the first spark of conscious reflection. The point of ignition grows larger. The fire spreads in ever widening circles till finally the whole planet is covered with incandescence. Only one interpretation, only one name can be found worthy of this grand phenomenon...outside and above the biosphere there is the noosphere.

It is in this collective mental cloud of rationalism and thought that we spend our existence. For the purposes of accomplishing a working of focused intent, this is not always beneficial. I refer to the collective constant press of mundane thought and psychic noise that impinges on each individual in the noosphere as *The Static*. It is the most pervasive and omnipresent of the external impediments to successful magical practice. It can be considered to be the antithesis of the state of vacuity. The Static is the sum of randomly received signals of all varieties via all senses, both mundane and magical. It is mental white noise that constantly bombards us. One of the reasons that some of the most effective magical workings are performed in the dead of night is simply because more people in your immediate vicinity are asleep, and thus not contributing as much of their discorant mental energy to the Static. Unopposed workings are always easier than opposed ones, and the cacophony of unfocused minds around you serves as de facto opposition.

An effective technique for counteracting The Static may be found in the principles of audio engineering. The process of noise cancellation involves broadcasting a signal that is the inverse waveform of an unwanted signal. The two waves interact in a process of destructive interference,

Voidworking

producing a composite signal. From a magical standpoint, this requires the development of a personal mental broadcast that cancels out the incident Static. This is a method that can be described, but not directly conveyed. It takes practice, and a perfect pattern for one person may well be useless for another. The exact nature and disposition of the Static in a given locale will also influence what type of countermeasure will be most effective. For example, the collective weight of fear, anxiety, and anger require more effort to neutralize than a general unfocused psychic babble does.

To learn what works best for you, begin by repeating syllables and patterns, common words, phrases, mantras, song lyrics, etc. This can be out loud or silently. The exercise is intended to occupy the mind with a loop, not to drown out any audible sounds. Even visualized patterns can be effective. Find something that is easy for you to maintain without a great deal of conscious thought. Practice your chosen pattern whenever you have a stray moment. The goal is to be able to invoke this signal whenever you wish, and then eventually to allow it to pass below the threshold of consciousness. Practice meditating in challenging conditions, such as among a noisy crowd to further develop your capability to neutralize any external distraction.

On the other end of the spectrum of impediments are the internal ones, which are often more daunting than the external. The best-known instance of this type is what is often referred to as the *Psychic Censor*. It is that part of our subconscious mind which performs the essential function of keeping us operating within consensus reality rather than frolicking with the machine elves or following the magic mirror to a nearby star system. Unfortunately, it also has the effect of nullifying magical operations by shutting them down via uncertainty and doubt like a disapproving parental figure:

"Magic isn't real, you must be crazy! Do the neighbors know you believe in that? Stop it."

The Censor must also be subverted for magic to be successful. Ironically, many of the same methods can be used to counteract *The Static* and the *Censor*. Inhibitory or excitatory states can work equally well. Ultimately, how this is done is irrelevant, as long as it is done. Calm your mind or blow it. Either way, banish The Static, and shatter the barriers that stand between you and seeing your will manifest. In the words of William S. Burroughs, "Exterminate all rational thought." This is one of the first and most essential acts of magic. It doesn't matter how many books you read, how many talismans you wear, or how many crystals you own. If you can't thwart your own inner voice telling you that you can't do magic, then you never *will* do magic.

I don't intend to be flippant in this observation. Overcoming a lifetime of skeptical thought is not easily done, but it can be accomplished via any number of methods. Perhaps the best of them all is simply to practice magic. Soak in it. Try diverse forms of it within myriad systems. All of them, including the one that I have been describing, are ultimately only tools. All functional magical systems are heuristic collections of gestures, terminology, and accouterments intended to facilitate the erosion of disbelief within the mind of the practitioner.

For getting past the Censor, many practitioners of Chaos Magic tend to emphasize a "fire and forget" approach to achieving a state of vacuity. Orgasm, exhaustion, hypoxia, and even hypothermia are only a few methods that I have encountered for blotting out the conscious mind and bypassing the skeptical subconscious in order to implant magical intent into emergent reality. I have found these types of techniques to be useful, and even edifying for immediate effects, but ultimately unsatisfying for the purpose of more complicated magical workings. For the latter purpose, I have espoused the approach of cultivating a persistent mindset more suited to if not assisting my practice, then at least standing down and staying out of the way of my Will.

Cultivating the appropriate mindset is both an instantaneous practice and a long-term concern. In order to perform magic, the mundane mode of existence must be set aside momentarily, but one must still be able to function in the mundane world.

The practice of magic requires the cultivation of the ability to focus on an idea with incredible intensity. Those who are incapable of this due to neurochemical circumstances may find this extremely difficult. This does not rule out magic for such individuals, it only means that they have a steeper climb ahead of them compared to their neurotypical peers. If you are in such a position, start by using whatever techniques that you already use to help you focus in your everyday life. Build on these techniques until you have a system that facilitates the level of focus that you require.

Regardless of your starting point, the process of refining your ability to tune your way of thinking will ultimately benefit you in myriad ways. In a world where so many people move through it without direction or forethought, you will render yourself into a force to be reckoned with simply by knowing what it is you wish to accomplish, and how to align your thoughts in a way best suited to achieve your goals.

Re-Imagining the Self

One of the privileges of taking up the practice of magic is the opportunity to effect profound changes in oneself. The construction of a magical personna is almost an essential aspect of the work. Naturally, the exact nature and disposition of this personality will be a combination of traits that you already possess, along with those you wish to cultivate.

An important aspect is the selection of your working name. This is the moniker by which you will be known as a worker of magic. It is what you will metaphorically carve into the universe to make it known that you were here. Some traditions and organizations may reserve the right to name you as they see fit. If that is acceptable to you, then so be it, but I've not long stayed affiliated with groups that hold this practice. It also may be possible that you use different names in different practices or organizations.

Sometimes the universe will serve you up a name by apparent coincidence, as it did in my case. Through a grave misunderstanding nearly three decades ago, I was named outlaw in a certain Asatru hearth's domain. In defiance, I in turn embraced the title and have used the moniker *Vargr23* ever since. It is thus possible that you may pick a name which you ultimately discard in favor of a more appealing one. Some may choose to keep their working name a secret. I however advocate the wide and unrestricted use of it. The wider the distribution of your name, the more traction you have in the phenomenal world to associate you with your persona.

If this is not advantageous to you due to your circumstances, you can also make the name known, but not your association with it. This renders it into a pseudonym under which to conceal your magical activities from employers, authorities, or unreceptive family members. There are numerous historical examples of this option, as practicing magic has been punishable by death in many times and places.

Selecting your working name is only part of the process. Envision your idealized self. What are the traits that you have? How do you interact with others? Do you speak differently? How do you dress? Are there personal role models that you wish to emulate? Make a list of the positive traits that you wish to obtain, and any negative existing ones that you wish to discard. The alchemical model of transformation might be a useful reference in this process, particularly the process of Conjunction. When you have an idea in mind of how it might feel to be this idealized self, start consciously attempting to adopt this new manor of behavior. Consider it akin to playing a role at first. As the beloved saying goes, "fake it til you make it." The more you enter into the mind space of your constructed persona, the easier it will become.

Some magicians choose to be their "magical self" only when actively performing a working. Others may find they choose to stay in this role in their mundane lives as well. It is also entirely possible that even if you do set this aspect of yourself aside, that traits from it will stick with you to some extent regardless.

The Nature and Use of Ritual

From a magical standpoint, a ritual can be thought of as being a set of actions, movements, and trappings that are used in concert with a prepared environment for the specific purpose of achieving a desired result. Timothy Leary's concept of "set and setting" for using psychedelics is an appropriate analogue of ritual. This is a narrower definition than a rite performed for religious purposes.

Ritual, whether simple or complex, can be a powerful tool in the practice of magic. There are several approaches as to the usefulness and nature of why this is so. If using a supernatural paradigm, then the technique can be thought to act as a mechanism by which higher or lower powers may be entreated to act on one's behalf. Within a materialist paradigm, ritual can be thought of as a tool by which subconscious desire may be better tuned and aligned towards accomplishing the goal of the working.

Depending on the nature and intent of the ritual, it may be gruelling, erotic, humorous, or banal. Whatever works best to cultivate the appropriate mindset to align with your purpose is what should be done. There are countless examples of pre-existing rituals that can be used either verbatim or after modification. These can also serve as inspirations for creating your own. Too, rituals may be constructed completely from scratch.

Many practitioners of chaos magic tend to denigrate the use of complex rituals, even as they perform countless small rituals at unawares. The process of creating a sigil or servitor is a ritual act, even if only a simple one. Freeform open-handed magic can be effective, but may not be able to bring as much intent to bear as a well-crafted ritual. As with magic in general, it is all a matter of intent and intensity.

I tend to categorize a ritual as complex if it includes props, tools, and special garments, as well as a workspace that has been in some way physically demarcated and decorated. The tools may be traditional such as the sword, wand, cup, etc. or of a personal nature. Appropriate colors, herbs, stones, and other corresponding elements can be combined to intensify the mood, as I will discuss in greater detail further on.

Acts of purification of the body, mind, or spirit may be required as part of the preparation for some rituals. These may include such practices as bathing in specific herbs, fasting, abstaining from sex, or engaging in acts of bodily mortification. Likewise, in contrast to avoiding them, the consumption of specific consecrated food, drinks, or other substances may also be a component of the preparation. The length of the period of preparation may vary, depending on the stipulations of the ritual. Most of these activities are designed to place the practitioner in a "pure" state, untainted by the profane, in order to enter into the ritual space. Exactly how much of this process is required will vary widely from individual to individual, or likewise between various groups or traditions.

Simple rituals may consist of basic incantations, or none at all, as well as only minimal trappings. These are often done on a more extemporaneous basis, especially if they are being done in immediate response to a crisis condition. The structure of these rituals is more fluid, and they may be performed with a lower degree of focus or mental investment. That being said, their effectiveness may be less than a more deliberate working, but still likely more than a simple sigil, simply due to a higher degree of focus of the Will that is applied through them.

Performing rituals that someone else has written is a good

place to start with, but as one advances in their magical practice, they will inevitably wish to create their own. As with all magical workings, it is necessary to first specify the intent of the ritual. What is the desired outcome for which it is to be performed? Further, once this is defined, you must consider what your criteria is for it to be considered a success. I'm certain that many magical practitioners may disagree with the latter, but in my experience it is a worthwhile exercise. If the ritual produces the desired outcome, then I am obviously more likely to incorporate it in my corpus for later re-use, whereas if it does not produce the desired result, I will typically tweak some aspect of it before trying it again. Ritual design is more of an art than a science, and like any chaotic system, introducing a minor change may produce a completely different result.

The basic aspects of a ritual may vary depending on its intent. There may be specific timing that is appropriate, such as on the new moon, or mid-winter's night, or simply at midnight for Void rituals. In contrast, there may be no specific time constraints at all. Following this determination is the selection of appropriate symbols and tools. What shall be used and how? Plain black trappings are appropriate, but a contrasting color must be selected for the construction of any sigils or general glyphs that are to be incorporated.

Once these details are nailed down, there is the matter of actually writing the text of the ritual. Is it to be read, or performed from memory? In cases of a repeating ritual, it may start as the former and become the latter. If there are movements or actions that participants are to perform, these must also be included. Treat it as if you are writing a short play, for indeed you are. You are the writer, choreographer, director, performer, and audience of your work. If the participants are numerous enough, one or two people should lead the others, giving them queues as needed. In hierarchical organizations, this is most often a senior leader of some type, but I've seen very moving rituals led by very talented novices that can rival a seasoned magus. It can also be useful to write practice rituals that are not actually intended to actually be performed, in order to get a better feel for appropriate complexity, pacing, etc.

The structure of the ritual can consist of a few basic components. Prior to its performance, each participant should engage in the specified preparation and purification that has been deemed appropriate. The ritual should start with a call to gather the participants, once they are gathered and garbed, into the appropriate space both physically and mentally. The demarcation/banishing of the working space should follow, to create a *Temporary Autonomous Zone* that is often referred to as *sacred space*. The invocation of any entities that are being petitioned should be performed immediately afterwards. This may be complex and serious, or something simply to the effect of "Hey universe, watch this!" The main body of the working, with appropriate speech and actions is next. This can include speaking in unison, repeating the words of the lead, or a structured call and response. This is where the magic happens, so to speak. You use the mindstate created

Voidworking

by your ritual to direct your collective Will, possibly enhanced by some entity or focus, to bring forth your desired end state. Afterwards, if you have invited powers to attend you, it is appropriate to thank them and take your leave. Do not be rude or dismissive of them. If an extra-dimensional sentient has deigned to attend your working, much less put its thumb on the cosmic scales on your behalf, it's best not to look down your nose at it. In conclusion, return your working space to its profane disposition.

Once all of the design is complete, all intended participants should perform at least one group read-through, and preferably several. Anyone with a speaking role should also be given ample opportunity to practice their lines solo. This process should be followed by at least one walk-through rehearsal. Everyone should know what role they are expected to play. This is all assuming that you desire a crisp, well-orchestrated end product. If this is not intended, then less preparation is necessary. My approach is that if I am going to take the time to write and orchestrate a ritual, then I want the greatest yield from it that can be obtained, so orderly performance is important. Others may prefer a more extemporaneous approach, and find that "doing it live" gives them better results. As in most endeavors, find what works best for you and use it.

After the ritual is complete, the participants should engage in some measure of cool-down and grounding together. Having a group meal can be an excellent exercise for this purpose. Even if performing a solo ritual, eating can help you fully re-integrate back into the mundane world.

The Importance of Symbols

The practice of sorcery can be thought of as the act of manipulating reality through the manipulation of symbols which are representative of various aspects and entities within that reality. In his seminal work *T. A. Z. - The Temporary Autonomous Zone, Ontological Anarchy, Poetic Terrorism*, Hakim Bey writes:

Sorcery works at creating around itself a psychic/physical space or openings into a space of untrammeled expression – the metamorphosis of quotidian place into angelic sphere. This involves the manipulation of symbols (which are also things) & of people (who are also symbolic)–the archetypes supply a vocabulary for this process & therefore are treated as if they were both real & unreal, like words.

Symbolic encoding can facilitate high-concept communication with the subconscious. In effect, it is easier to grasp any given concept if it can be rendered into a shorthand form. There are countless symbols already in existence, of both magical and mundane origins that can be used, adapted and co-opted. For example, I have used schematic circuit diagrams and meteorological markers to good effect.

Besides assembling a personal collection of ready-to-use symbols, investigation of the topic can lead to greater comfort and skill in the creation of one's own personal set of permanent and ephemeral tools. An in-depth study of semiotics is beyond the scope of this work, but I recommend the works of Ferdinand de Saussure, Roland Barthes, and Jacques Derrida as a launching point for a solid foundation in its principles.

Besides encoding a meaning that can be pushed to a sublingual part of the mind, the symbol itself can serve as a distraction to the conscious mind. The complexity of some of the symbols of the Hermetic corpus is impressive. Through the process of creating the components of a complicated symbol, the mind is immersed in its meaning such that it becomes more easily subsumed by the subconscious. The skill of learning how you best internalize information is worth cultivating in order to best take advantage of this exposure.

Austin Osman Spare applied the technique of symbolic encoding in several ways. Perhaps his best known method, beloved for decades by chaos magicians, was that of forming sigils from the non-repeating consonants of one's statement of intent. Another was via his Alphabet of Desire, or the encoding of sensations into symbols. Spare's methods can also be applied to individual words or phrases. Personal connotation is an essential component of this process. If you use a synthesized language of barbarous words, the ciphers themselves can be further distilled into glyphs which can be written or inscribed for any desired purpose. This intensified obfuscation of meaning can keep the rational mind from interfering with the work.

For purposes of clarity, I use the term *sigil* to refer specifically to a spell of symbolic manipulation after the manner of Spare, which I explored in detail on in *Quantum Sorcery*. For more general magical symbols, I also use the term *glyph*. This nomenclature is somewhat arbitrary, but it can be useful to be able to distinguish between these concepts.

Symbolizing the Self

With an understanding of the utility of symbolic encoding, it follows that it is therefore essential to create a symbol that represents the self. If a complex symbolic image is used in the casting of a spell, one to attract wealth, for example, what better way to represent that the self is to be the recipient than to include this personal proxy in the encoding of the spell? Even as each demon and spirit has a seal that represents it, so should a magical worker. This can be used not only in physical forms, but visualized as a symbol of your will and your work in virtual and astral spaces.

Once you have created your symbol, use it as often as possible, until it becomes second nature to you as much as your chosen working name is. Imbue it with your Will. Create a representation of it in your temple or on your altar. Engrave it upon your working tools. If you have an apprentice, mark them with it in some manner, whether physically or virtually to indicate to the Universe that they are under your protection and tutelage. You and your symbol should be synonymous with one another. It is not intended to be a protected secret, but rather a calling card. Put everything that you can muster into it whenever you can. Make it such that hostile powers tremble in its presence.

The Glyph of the Void

Even as any sorcerer should have a personal glyph, so should the Void itself be assigned one for use in magical works. There is no universally recognized symbol for this concept, which necessitates the assignment of one for this purpose. One possibility is the mathematical notation of the *empty set*:

From the boundless aspect of the Void, the infinity symbol might also suffice:

Neither of these appealed to me, so I endeavored to create a personal symbol for my own use. The following symbol emerged from a session of meditation and automatic writing. It is in some ways evocative of a stroke of black lightning, which traverses a threshold from above to below. You can use this symbol, or use an appropriate method either via random or specific design techniques to develop one of your own. As with any magical glyph, it can then be inscribed on an appropriate medium for use as a talisman or meditation focus, or combined with your own personal symbol to create a magical link between yourself and the Void.

The Glyph of the Void

The Primal Vortex

Why the Void first stirred cannot be known, yet there are many conflicting beliefs in mythology that assert to explain how this occurred. As I have explored before, some say that it was stirred by the will and action of a god, while others believe that the potential in the Void self-motivated without an external stimulus. In any case, for the purpose of this evocation, I emphasize the nature of the Void as fluid in nature. When a fluid is stirred, it is common for vortices to form. A vortex is most simply defined as the flow of a fluid around an axis. This phenomenon is manifest at all scales, from cream stirred into coffee, to hurricanes, to the accretion disks of matter that form around black holes. This conceptual symbol can be used in a number of ways in Voidworking, particularly for the purpose of gathering energy, as action occurs from apparent stillness.

Voidworking

I conceive that the first perturbation of the Void resulted in the creation of the first vortex, against which all others are but pale imitations of its Platonic perfection. I name this primal movement *ION*, loosely translated from the Greek for *that which moves*. That is my god-form. It is inhuman, and insentient, but it is in motion. It is in fact the first and oldest motion. It is not an elemental entity, as it predates the existence of the elements. Like tornadoes and hurricanes, it is neither good nor evil. It is a force of nature outside nature.

After years spent in pursuit of logos within a number of pagan faiths, I have come to embrace the idea that ultimately one should only truly trust the deities that are created by oneself. Having a god or goddess to call on in ritual and magical work can be useful, but the various ones typically engaged all have various degrees of baggage, so to speak. Are you invoking what you think you are? I know the attributes and behavior of my deity. It can be dangerous, destructive, and capricious, but it is also a source of immense energy. I tap into this energy in order to add its potency to my magical workings. I do not pray to it or worship it as such, but whenever I encounter a vortex out in the world, typically a dust devil full of dead leaves, I incant 'Io ION!', and mark it as a sign of good fortune.

My somatic trigger for tapping into the potential of ION is very simple. I point my right index finger, perpendicular to the ground, and make a circular stirring motion with it. I begin slowly, then gradually increase the speed of the rotation. This motion is accompanied by a simple chant: "Io ION, Io ION, one who moves, one who moves." This simple technique can be effective for accompanying basic acts of open-hand magic, such as attempting to influence a sudden and unexpected situation.

The glyph of ION is a sigil of its letters, styled after the hurricane warning symbol used in some weather maps. It's form reflects its function.

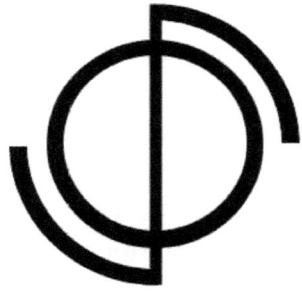

The Glyph of ION

Emanations of the Void

Entities evoked from the Void can be envisioned in any number of ways, either as exiled beings from other possible realities as in *Imajica* or as indigenous dwellers in the darkness described in other games or fictional works. These are a distinct category as compared to Dee and Crowley's demon *Choronzon*, who is not seen as being at the behest of any mortal magician.

In order to bring forth an emanation of the Void, start by

Voidworking

visualizing its form and function. Create a list of its attributes. Give it a name and a symbol by which it can be called and controlled (or revered as in the case of nascent godforms like ION). This is the most vital step in the process of evocation. A thing named is a thing created. The actual initial manifestation will be akin to a *Tulpa* or thoughtform. Too, a physical icon or symbol which serves as an anchor for the entity is recommended to reinforce its existence.

Repeated evocation (or invocation if appropriate) will increase the persistence of your creation. An in-depth treatment of the care and feeding of such entities is beyond the scope of this work, but there are numerous existing sources that even a cursory search will produce. In brief, such entities will thrive on receiving attention and thus mental/magical energy as with any synthesized emanation. A temporal parameter may be useful to assign during the manifestation of these entities. How long do you want it to continue to exist before being subsumed by the Void?

The manifestation of Void entities can be taxing to undertake, and such beings once instantiated can also function as psychic parasites if care is not taken during their construction to forestall such behavior. Effective possession of the magician by the entity of their own design can be the ultimate result of such a circumstance in the most extreme of cases. For this reason, one should be thoroughly familiar with effective techniques of shielding and banishing before undertaking this type of work, as well as having a definitive technique specifically for the disposal of the emanation.

Not all constructs of the Void need be seen as sentient or motile. Nor is it always the case that the mind of the mage is the motivation in their emergence. Although most who work with them have likely never considered the idea, it is implied in the *Prose Edda* that the Runes emerged from the unknown depths below the roots of Yggdrasil. Odin perceived them only after nine days of hanging upon the tree in a self-initiatory ordeal. He did not create them, they existed in an archetypal state of unrealized potential until he seized them and brought them back into the nine worlds. This concept is also found in the theory of Platonic forms. Before an image is manifest in the mind, it resides in the Void, waiting to be pulled forth.

One need not go to the lengths that Odin did in order to perceive forms and bring them forth into our world. Much as *terma*, or hidden teachings are thought to be discovered in Tibetan Buddhist traditions, a sorcerer can, through meditation, ritual, and study, receive forms from the Void. A contemporary example of this is the *Ashe* calligraphic stroke received by Chogyam Trungpa Rinpoche, founder of the Shambhala movement. In fact, the previously described *Glyph of the Void* is itself one of these forms. In order to instantiate such a form, you must first conceptualize your need. Focus on its essence and then cast this distilled thought out into the Void as a message in a bottle is thrown into the sea. Wait for a form to be returned to you, and record it as best you can in whatever medium is appropriate. It may be visual, audible, somatic, or some combination of these modalities. The actual method of reception may be accomplished via the meditation and scrying techniques described later in this book.

Such forms may be fragmentary, or require progressive attempts to grasp, or they may be fully realized upon initial discovery. Once the actual form is discerned, its nature must then be ascertained as well. This too may be either quickly done or may require some period of time. Is it exactly what you asked for? Is it more or less, or slightly different than what you thought you needed? If so, this may be serendipitous rather than a failure. Do not be discouraged if your initial attempts are unsatisfactory. The skill of retrieval and interpretation will increase with practice as with any other. I suggest starting with simple concepts or needs in order to develop an affinity for the technique.

Keep a record of everything that you receive through the application of this technique. This can result in the development of your own Alphabet of Desire which you can draw upon in order to create spells of your own design.

Gods and Monsters

Not all who wish to use a godform in their magic will want to undergo the creation of a persistent entity as I do. Some may prefer the comfort of using existing divinities from various mythos. In this case, there are many beings that may serve this purpose. Although deities of death or of the underworld might be used for such, the Void is not inherently the realm of the dead. It should be thought of rather as the domain of that which has not yet been brought into being. In this light, my best recommendation is to go back as close to the origin of all that is known as possible. In Greek mythology, as described by Hesiod and other sources, Chaos itself produced two relevant offspring at the foundation of the firmament, those being *Erebus*, or Darkness, and *Nyx*, or Night.

There are few surviving myths in which Erebus appears. He is described as little more than a personification of darkness itself, and as the husband of his sister Nyx, father of *Hemera*, or day, and *Aither*, or light with her. More material survives on Nyx. She is depicted in several forms, one of which is a beautiful woman shrouded in dark mist. In addition to her children with Erebus, she spawned a number offspring including death, pain, and strife. Despite the nature of her get, she is not described as an inherently evil goddess. To work with her is to truly embrace the night in its most primordial form. Her symbol is the moon, and correspondingly the moonstone is thought to be sacred to her.

In antiquity, neither of these deities is known to have had large followings, or dedicated temples, but they were revered by some. There is no reason that either or both could not be called on for workings involving concealment, darkness, or shadow. Further, if one were prepared to work with the dearth of dogmatic material, either might be professed as a patron deity.

Voidworking

In Babylonian mythology, another highly applicable deity is found in Tiamat, the primordial serpent goddess that was slain by Marduk. As described in *Enûma Elish*, the Babylonian creation myth, Tiamat was the personification salt-water sea which intermingled with Apsu, the freshwater sea, and thus begot the balance of the gods. In addition, she also spawned all manner of serpents and monsters when she went to war with her descendants. After her destruction, Marduk fashioned heaven and earth from her body. Tiamat was originally opposed to conflict with her get, but Apsu could not abide their clamor, and was goaded by his vizier, Mummu, to destroy them. Tiamat and Apsu's great grandson Ea saw through the plan, and subdued Apsu with a sleep incantation and subsequently slew him. It was only then that Tiamat desired to make war against the other gods. She is a primal creative feminine force, who came to be demonized and destroyed by a later masculine force. This is only one such instance of this phenomenon of supposed order defeating chaos to occur in magico-religious systems throughout the world over the millennia. To put it bluntly, she got a raw deal and a bum rap.

A related serpentine entity which is not itself a deity, yet might be useful in Void workings is the world-serpent. One of the oldest known conceptions of this being was *Ouroboros*, or "Tail-eater" found in Egyptian magical and funerary works dating as far back as the 14th century BC. In this guise, it symbolizes the chaos that surrounds the world, as well as the boundary between the ordered and unordered states of existence. The Norse named this serpent *Jormungandr*, and foretold that it would poison the seas and the skies at the time of Ragnarok. Used as a boundary symbol, the *Ouroboros* can serve as a microcosmic representation of its larger nature, separating the work of the magician from the profane realm without. Like Choronzon, it may be bested and banished in order to access or transcend the Void it demarcates. Mastery over this entity implies the capability of determining the extent of the limits of reality.

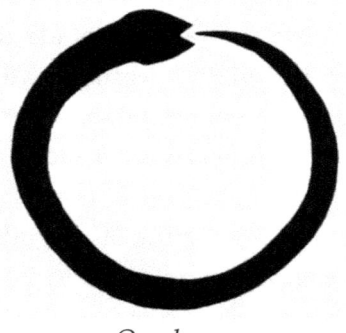

Ouroboros

In the Tibetan Buddhist practice of Vajrayana, there is another highly applicable spirit that can be worked with. This is *Troma Nagmo*, sometimes called the Black Dakini. She is the wrathful goddess of the Void. She is a fierce and harsh feminine aspect, but she also brings wisdom to those who are not afraid to cast aside their path and professions to pursue her. The teachings of her path to liberation are closely held and not freely shared. Nubile, with three eyes and black skin, she is often compared to the Hindu goddess Kali.

If you choose to work with a particular deity, then you should attempt to learn everything that you can about them. This will serve both to best understand their ascribed nature, and to be aware of any pitfalls that may arise from such practice.

Visualization

The most critical component of performing any kind of magic is visualization. You must be able to see your workings in your mind's eye, using whatever internal symbol set or paradigm that you find best suits your needs. To put it bluntly, you have to imagine it. The idea of visualization is one that many magical systems tend to shy away from, as if we can all conjure luminous plasma or manifest violet flames from our hands at will. Visualization is not a diversion from the practice of successful magic. It is rather the essential internal precursor to external manifestation. In order to make your will manifest in the phenomenal world, you must be able to see it executed to fruition in your own mind's eye. I assert that this is the open secret of the Hermetic principle of magic. The classical magical systems of the east and west offer a plethora of frameworks, as do modern occult works. Besides these "traditional" sources, there are countless examples of ostensibly fictional systems in books, films, comics, and video games. Find a framework that suits your needs and desires or synthesize your own. The provenance of your system is not as important as its effectiveness.

All of the meditational practices that I've outlined later in the book can be used as starting points for calming and training the mind in order to better practice visualization.

Practically any contemplative practice will also suffice. One of the first exercises that I was taught was to picture a simple white-glazed vase. To see its shape, its curves, it's reflectance. It was like seeing an object in virtual reality. I pictured it countless times, noting how the aging of the glaze had caused a fine pattern of cracks across its surface. Over time, I refined the resolution of my view. To follow this practice, think of a simple object that you will focus on. It can be something that you already have an affinity for, or something random. Once you have it, practice visualizing it. Do it often. Do it until it bores you. Do it until it is second nature, and you know every detail of your object.

Voidworking in Practice

Now that an operating definition of the Void has been established, and some of the basic tenets of magical practice have been enumerated, it is time to move past theory into practice, and to delve into Voidworking proper. This is a collection of techniques that I have used that exemplify some of the ways that the Void can be used in practical magical workings. This is not intended to convey the full width and breadth of ways that the Void can be utilized. I encourage you to use these offerings as an inspiration for your own exploration of the topic, with the hope that you realize the potential of this system.

The nature of the Void is emptiness and unformed potential. It is fluid and protean. Related concepts of dissolution, darkness, shadow, and a sense of sinking or

Voidworking

falling are recurring themes in these workings. Magic that hinges on an element of the Void will tend towards these modalities. This magic is also concerned with evoking and ordering forms and emanations. This is not a technique of probability or subtle influence as are some forms of sorcery. It is generally not well-suited to matters of love or healing, although there may be applications in these spheres.

Tools, Trappings, and Correspondences

There are no specific set of magical working tools or directional/elemental correspondences specified in the Voidworking paradigm. At minimum a tool to assist in the projection of focused will is suggested, but even this is ultimately unnecessary if you are comfortable doing this technique open-handed. If there are tools that you are comfortable with from other working traditions, by all means use them here too. Everyone eventually collects a certain set of tools, symbols, and techniques that resonate most strongly for them. It's foolhardy to discard such affinity in favor of tradition.

When appropriate to the working, the selection of appropriate tools and trappings will provide a greater sense of connection to the working, as well as a deeper investment of intent. Too, the utilization of colors, scents, stones, and other decorations of the altar and work space can set the mood. Note that if you are working with specific godforms or spirits, then using the traditional symbology, colors, and scents associated with those entities is preferred, as you are attempting to align your set and setting with that entity rather than your own aesthetic.

Color has been found to have a profound effect on human mood and emotional state. It stands to reason that this effect should apply to magical workings as well. The most prominent color used in Void magic should (obviously?) be black, preferably matte rather than gloss if possible. Black by definition is the color that represents the absorption or absence of all visible light. It is the most natural color of correspondence for the Void. It denotes power and mystery, and has long been the color of magic in general. As a complementary dark color, burgundy works well. It evokes a feeling of sophistication and gravitas. For a contrasting hue, silver and bright red are both good choices. The former is indicative of all things mercurial and lunar, whereas the latter embodies the boldness of both passion and anger.

Building on this foundation, it is easy to assemble a list of corresponding black tools and trappings. Black knives and candles, crow feathers, obsidian, onyx, and ashes all have their place in this paradigm. Black banners or tapestries that feature images or icons that are evocative of the Void, or even simple cloth can be used to adorn walls and furniture within the working space. Not everyone has the luxury of a dedicated temple or magical working space, but you should at least have an altar of some kind, whether permanent or ephemeral. I am now fortunate enough to have a room dedicated to my practice, but for many years of my magical practice, I kept my tools and trappings in a box and only set them up when it was time to perform a working.

Following the physical design of the space, there are certain scents that lend themselves to establishing an appropriate setting as well. Night-blooming flowers such as night queen/lotus, moon flowers, and night-blooming jasmine, or tree resins such as copal and myrrh for a heavier mood. In general, whatever aspects best create a physical and mental space most suited to the performance of your magic is what should be used.

Clothing and jewelry that are used only for esoteric purposes can advance this effect even farther. None of these must themselves be elaborate, but they should not be shabby. When appropriate to the ritual, I wear a simple hooded black robe, with a plain black leather belt closed by a wrought-iron buckle. I accompany this with an Ouroboros medallion, or occasionally others as suits the nature of the work. It is easy to obtain suitable garb commercially if you have no capability or desire to produce it yourself. As with other tools, every aspect of ritual garb should support the magic being performed. Nothing that can detract from the mindset should be used. The input of every sense should be pervaded with the appropriate stimuli. It is difficult enough to impose one's Will upon the universe under the best of circumstances, and every advantage that can be had should be taken.

Void Stones

One working tool that I have found to be useful is what I

call a *Void Stone*. Mine is a two-inch diameter black onyx sphere, which nests on a base of the same material. This is not glossy, like those that are used for scrying, but rather has quite a dull finish. This piece acts as a microcosmic representation of the Void itself. It is the anchor of my Voidworking. It also makes an excellent grounding stone. It seems to eat anxious and nervous energy, and radiate back a much calmer frequency.

To consecrate your own Void Stone, first obtain an appropriate piece of stone. It need not be of any particular size or shape, although regular geometric shapes such as spheres or pyramids may prove to be more satisfying than a mere rough piece of stone. An egg-shape may be especially effective. Likewise, it need not be of any particular variety, but jet, onyx, and obsidian are all good candidates. Each type of stone has different attributes traditionally associated with it, and there are numerous sources available for learning these. In general, black stones are receptive, defensive, and stable in nature. Finding a specimen that appeals to you is more important for the purpose of this tool than the folklore of the material.

Place the stone in a prominent place on your altar. Light a heavy-scented incense. Demarcate your working space in a manner that suits you. Stand or sit before it and focus all of your attention on the stone, such that all else fades into the background, then speak the following incantation:

As this stone is a shard of the earth
Let it now be a mote of the Void

Fragment of the ineffable
Gateway to the formless realm
Wellspring of unlimited potential
Until all that is
Is unmade
By my Will it is done
It is done
It is done

The stone will thenceforth serve as your symbolic link that can be used to increase the effectiveness of any work involving the Void. If it is not to be left on your altar, then keep it in a bag of black cloth or leather. If it is small enough, you may choose to carry your stone on your person, and perhaps even use it as a worry-stone. You might find it to be advantageous to create more than one stone in order to facilitate this, particularly if your primary is very large.

Black Water

The Void is fluid in nature, and thus it is only fitting that a fluid can be used to symbolize it in magical workings. Although commercially obtained black vodka can be used for this purpose, it is better to prepare your own medium. As is the case with any magical tool, the intent that is invested into its creation can only be beneficial when it comes to producing results. This *Black Water* can be made through a number of methods. Five drops of Sumi or India ink can be added to eight ounces of water to produce a suitable solution. Either will suffice, but I have found that India ink stays mixed longer. Another option is to dissolve a tablespoon of activated charcoal powder in ounces of water. Charcoal powder can be obtained at some pharmacies or online from numerous vendors. If this method is used, it will likely be necessary to shake up the fluid more often if you wish it to remain opaque, as the charcoal will precipitate out of the solution. In my experience, the ink method produces a more stable and opaque result, which also keeps a smooth, mirrored surface.

The water that is used to create the black fluid may also carry significance if desired. I typically use hallowed distilled water, but you could use rainwater, meltwater from snow or hailstones (my favorite), or even water from a sacred spring. Be as elaborate with this as you wish or need to be. For my part, I add a pinch of black salt to the water in addition to the blackening agent.

Once created, this fluid serves several purposes. It can be used to fill a vessel for scrying, in the creation of Black Jars, or frozen to use in Black Ice magic. Each of these techniques will be discussed later.

Hallowing

Any tool or material that is to be used in a magical working should first be hallowed to its purpose. This is not a dedication to any particular deity, but rather to your own Will. This sets it apart from the mundane world, and bestows it with magical potential. A very simple ritual for accomplishing this purpose follows:

Hold the item, take a deep breath, and exhale upon it. As you do so, envision your vitality permeating it and engulfing it. Speak the following:

I hallow this <object> to my purpose.
Let it be imbued with my Will.

If you wish to purify it further, smudge the item with sage or juniper smoke.

Once you have thus dedicated your tools and materials, it is best not to let others handle them. They have been rendered sacred to you, and should be treated as such. This reinforces the association of the object with the exertion and fulfilment of your Will.

Banishing

In magical terms, the concept of banishing refers to the act of dismissing undesired entities or energies. This can be done directly against a specific entity, or to a delineated space to clear it of all unwanted influences and energies, and to create a null space that is ready for ritual activities. In the case of the former usage, the entity in question can be thought of as anything from a sentient agent to an embodied emotional or mental state that has been manifest specifically to be rid of it. I recommend the use of some type of banishing prior to the performance of any other magical working or ritual beyond the simplest of open-handed working. The benefit of this is psychological as well as arcane. It primes you and prepares your mind for what is to follow.

I follow a straightforward process for establishing a space. First, declare the entity or entities under whose authority the space is to be created. It may be one or more deities, or it may be simply by the exertion of your own power. Next is the actual definition of the space. You may draw or pace a circle on the ground, or simply use a tool to project your envisioned boundary. In some instances that I have seen, a working group will mark the floor of their temple with gaffer tape. The definition of the space may involve asperging with consecrated water or even blood. Elemental or angelic presence may be called upon at the cardinal directions. After defining the physical extent of the space, you must define its purpose. This may be specific to a particular working, or just a general assertion of authority to tweak the rules of reality within it. This general structure provides a good framework for the creation of your own procedure.

Some workers assume that a space is essentially inviolable once established, and that if one must leave it, then a "cutting out" of the circle must be performed. Rather than this stricture, I use the analogy that the sacred space is like a bubble. One may freely enter with the permission of the creator. If one must pass outside of the threshold for some reason, then the space stretches to encompass them like a membrane with an umbilicus. If they re-enter the space, this extension is simply re-absorbed. If they do not return, or move a sufficient distance away, the extension simply pulls back from around them, and retracts like an amoeba.

Voidworking

You should decide the parameters of your own particular space prior to creating it.

Some magical spaces are permanent in nature, and are never dissolved once they are created. This may include a temple or lodge working space, a sacred grove, etc. Most are temporary, and are intended for a finite use. This latter type must be dispelled once it is no longer of use. The method by which this is done, both physically and metaphysically is dependent on its creation. If you are using candles or torches to define your boundary, obviously these must be extinguished. If you are using a length of cord to form a circle, it must be retrieved, and so forth. If you have invited the overwatch of evoked entities, then they should be respectfully released in an appropriate manner. In short, the space must be released back into the larger world.

In *Quantum Sorcery* I introduced my standard banishing technique for claiming a ritual working space. I use it prior to doing any work in my own temple. I envision the result of performing this to be more of a *Temporary Autonomous Zone* than a traditional Sacred Space. Since I first began using this method, more than ten years ago, I have streamlined it slightly. The current incarnation of it follows.

Start with the feet shoulder-width apart, arms hanging loosely with the dagger held in your dominant hand. Take several deep breaths. Raise the projecting arm until it is parallel to the ground, pointing straight out in front of you.

Dave Smith

By my Will I cleave the dimensions.

Sweep your arm down and across your body until your blade is pointing at the ground on the opposite side. Visualize the fabric of mundane reality parting under your stroke. Return your arm to its starting, pointing position. Turn in place counter-clockwise, sweeping the blade in a 360-degree motion, parallel to the ground. Envision the reach of your influence extending to the walls of your temple, or otherwise describing a circle of desired radius.

I claim this space from the Void.

End this horizontal sweep back at the starting position. Sweep the point backwards over your shoulder, perpendicular to the ground, somewhat like performing a backstroke.

Within this domain, I am the alpha...

as your blade is pointing straight up

...and the omega.

as your blade is pointing straight down.

So mote it be,

Finish the sweep with your blade held pointing up, held in front of your face, as in a fencing salute. Sweep both arms down until they are held out from your sides, pointing at the ground at a 45-degree angle from your body,

My Will be done.

By this simple incantation, along with the physical act of delineating the space with a dagger or sword, I am creating my own personal slice of reality, claimed from the Void itself. It doesn't take a god to establish a realm of order from the chaos of the as-of-yet unmade. I do it every time I perform ritual magic. I embrace the Void and carve out my own pocket universe. I destroy it in turn when its purpose has been fulfilled, relinquishing my dominion over it and returning the space to its mundane state. This is done by a simple statement:

I release this space from my dominion. Let me (us) re-integrate into the most advantageous time-stream and go forth to work my (our) Will.

The bubble that was carved out is thus returned to the Void.

Besides this general practice of creating a working space, a more direct and aggressive banishing technique can be applied directly to entities whose presence is undesired. Following is an example of this type of incantation:

By the might of my Will,
I purge your stain from this world.
I consign you to oblivion.
I name you Anathema
I cast you into the Void.
Zax Kazos Kabestat Vakos

All undesired things can be consigned to the Void. Unwanted emotions such as anger, sorrow, envy, love, or hate. Likewise, physical sensations such as pain can be dealt with in this manner. All of these concepts can be envisioned and evoked as entities in and of themselves, and as such, they can be detached from the self and pushed into the dissolution of nothingness. In order to easier facilitate the use of this technique on a mind state, such as anxiety, it can be useful to personify them through the creation of a symbol to represent it, similar to the seals of the Enochian spirits recorded by John Dee.

Meditating on the Void

Void meditation is a calming practice done to increase ones affinity for the emptiness of the Void. It can be performed as a preparation to ritual work, which I highly recommend, as well as an activity in its own right. It is best done in a darkened or dimly lit space. In a seated and upright position, either on a cushion with legs folded, or in a chair with feet firm on the ground, place your hands palms down on your legs, just above the knees. Unfocus or close your eyes, whichever you prefer. Ensure that your spine is straight, but try to release other tension from the shoulders and neck by rolling the head back and forth from side to side, always forward. Follow this by rolling the shoulders simultaneously forward several times, and then backwards several more. Your mouth should be open slightly, while pressing your tongue lightly against the roof of your mouth, with the tip just behind your teeth. Breathe in and out deeply, but do not exaggerate your breathing. Relax. Begin to feel yourself sinking down into a strongly rooted position on the earth, while visualizing a vast and empty space above you, devoid of all light or disturbance. Continue to breathe deeply and easily as this feeling intensifies. Feel your awareness expand into this space. Time and space lose their relevance for the moment, and all tellurian matters recede into the background. If a mantra is desired, consider repeating the following:

The Void is empty, I am the Void.
The Void is formless, I am the Void.
The Void is boundless, I am the Void.
The Void is endless, I am the Void.

I refer to this sequence as the "Attributes of the Void".

Another highly appropriate audible component is to intone Sanskrit or Tibetan mantras if you know them. There are many which specifically relate to emptiness, and the act of consciousness emanating forth from it. An example of this is the aptly named *Mantra of Emptiness*. Another possibility is the use appropriate synthetic, so-called *barbarous* words, also known as *voces magicae*. These are nonsense words that are used as cyphers for words or even complete phrases in incantations in some flavors of Chaos Magic. An example of these is the final phrase in the banishing incantation above:

Zax / Kazos / Kabestat / Vakos = by the power / of my will / profane ones / depart

After the phrase is constructed and rendered into this

obfuscated form, the rational meaning becomes decoupled from the words, and interference in the working by the 'rational' mind can be minimized. Ringing words with hard consonants and long vowels lend themselves well to the purpose.

Repeat the mantra as desired out loud, then begin to lower your voice as you do so, until you are finally mouthing the words without sound, and then repeating them only in your mind.

When you have reached the desired state of calmness and expansion of yourself into the emptiness, enjoy this sensation for as long as you wish. You may feel a peaceful floating sensation, akin to a sensory deprivation tank or a warm bath. When you are ready to leave this state, begin to pull your awareness back into the space behind your eyes, until your focus is entirely returned to the present moment. Before opening your eyes, simply listen to the space around you. Feel the air that surrounds you. Your senses will be heightened. At last, open your eyes. Recite the following to conclude your session:

I am the space between the stars
I am that from which all forms originate
And to which all that is shall return
I am the Void.

Disintegration

Once an operating level of comfort has been achieved with

Voidworking

the basic Void Mediation, the pursuit of more advanced techniques can proceed. I refer to the next practice as the process of *Disintegration*. This visualization envisions the dissolution of the self into the Void, followed by the re-emergence of an altered self, purified of static and mental detritus. When first practicing this technique, it is not unusual to feel fleeting moments of a falling sensation, as if falling in a dream. This may cause a shock, or a start that may interrupt the process. Do not be discouraged by this if it occurs. Over time, this sensation will lessen in severity, or cease altogether. Visualization is a key skill in the practice of magic, but visualizing nothingness can be more challenging than anticipated.

Imagine yourself standing on a matte black surface, perfectly smooth and featureless, and extending in all directions as far as you can perceive. The sky above you is a uniform gunmetal grey. There is an ambient light, as the sun behind thick clouds.
By your own will, you begin to sink slowly into the surface. As you are subsumed, you begin feeling lighter and lighter. The more of you that sinks into the inky blackness, the lighter you become. As your mouth passes below the surface, you drink in the darkness, freely allowing it to fill you. There is no panic, only serenity and acceptance. As the top of your head ultimately disappears below the perfect smoothness of the plain, there is no evidence left of your having been there. Your consciousness expands and diffuses throughout the lightless material. As it does so, your awareness expands to encompass a vast volume. The passage of time slows for you. This sensation

continues at an easy pace, without any sense of urgency, until you reach a state of restful equilibrium. Stay in this state as long as you wish.

When it is time to reconstitute yourself, feel your consciousness begin to coalesce back into yourself. As it does so, disruptive elements of thought that are detrimental to your working are filtered out, and left behind in the darkness, much as water is purified as it passes through charcoal. As you reform, you begin to slowly re-emerge from the surface of the black plain. Your focus is sharper, your thoughts are coherent. All undesired magical attachments and parasitic connections have been stripped away. All mental static has been left behind in the void. You are a blank slate, ready to receive and actualize intent. You are now ready for whatever ritual undertaking you desire.

The Rite of Erasure

A variation of the disintegration technique can also serve as an offensive working. Rather than yourself, visualize your adversary sinking into the surface of impenetrable darkness. As they sink, their faculties are inhibited, their own magical capabilities are constrained, and they are rendered incapable of action. The visualization should also be accompanied by an incantation:

<Name of your adversary>
Thrice accursed
You are doomed and damned

Sink down!
Never to rise
Until you are loosed
All is darkness
All is still
You are erased from the realm of light
You are bound in the realm of shadows

An appropriate glyph, evocative of sinking can be carved into a slender black candle, accompanied by a glyph representing the target, preferably closer to the wick. As the flame burns past and consumes the symbols of intent, your adversary is consigned to their fate. Should you desire to reverse this spell, inscribe your original glyph inverted on a white candle, along with the adversary's symbol, and allow it to burn down until it is obliterated. When an entity is consigned to oblivion, it is not destroyed. Its essence is merely dissolved and diffused. Nothing is ever truly destroyed, only transformed.

A Glyph of Sinking

Additionally, if you possess any linking objects to your target, such as a lock of hair, swatch of cloth that they have worn, or even a photograph, these can be burned, and the ashes collected and kept. This will potentially cause a more effective result of this incantation. If you desire to reverse your working, pour the ashes into flowing water. I include this aspect of the spell, as I advise against the use of irreversible offensive workings, It is possible that your perspective and disposition toward your target may change. Over time, you may learn information that you did not know when you initially took action. Indeed, one-time foes may become allies under the right circumstances. Know also that when you perform this type of malediction, the act creates a magical link between yourself and the recipient. This is another aspect of the Abyss gazing back into you. In many cases, the drain upon yourself that can result from this type of working is absolutely worth the risk, but be wary and judicious in the use of these techniques.

Extending this aspect of the working farther, any emotional state, sensation, or aspect of being can be personified, and then caused to be consigned to Erasure. I have on various occasions visualized and symbolized chronic pain as an entity, and then banished it to the Void via this technique. As described in the previous banishing, sorrow, anger, and loneliness, or even unwanted love might likewise be ameliorated.

A unique glyph to represent the concept should be created, as with any other entity. This can then be used along with the glyph of sinking, burned, placed in a ritual jar etc.
Once again, the creation and imbuement of a symbol with the appropriate attributes is key to a successful working.

Voidworking

If you operate within a paradigm that utilizes extradimensional or supernatural entities, these beings are equally susceptible to this working. If they can be represented by a name and a symbol, then they can be made to sink into oblivion and be erased from the sunlit world. Again, the greater the amount of information that you can assemble on your target, the more likely you will succeed in your actions against them. Some traditions esteem the knowledge of a so-called True Name to be able to work against an entity. Such information might be gained through extensive scrying, dream-work or the like, but is ultimately outside of practical reach. My typical practice is to look for the oldest given name for an entity that I can find. Existing grimoires, mythology, and even historical records can all be valuable sources. With the increasing number or works that are being digitized and made freely available online, this type of research is easier than at any prior point in human history. Even as we weep for the Library of Alexandria, we have greater resources at our disposal. This is the dichotomy of practicing magic in the information age.

The Black Jar

Besides the candle method, the Erasure of your adversary can also be performed by means of a Black Jar. The use of magic jars, sometimes referred to as Witch Bottles is prevalent in western folk magic, and they can be potent. A detailed discussion of all of their possible configurations is beyond the scope of this work, but the general principle is that ingredients that are sympathetic to the desired magical effect are collected in a jar or bottle, possibly along with an appropriate liquid, such as urine, vinegar, honey, hot sauce, or simple water. After it is sealed, the jar is sometimes hidden or buried. In some instances, a small bottle may also be worn as a talisman.

To create a Black Jar, first select an appropriate container. It should be clear glass with a tight seal, such that you can see the fluid within, and can shake the container without spilling its contents. Decorate the body and lid as you see fit. One possibility is to place your own seal on the top of the lid. Fill the glass with black liquid, either the previously described Black Water or black vodka, which is also a good medium for this purpose. Add a pinch of black salt to your liquid. Write the appropriate name and symbol on a piece of paper or parchment. Be as elaborate as you see fit. Obtain a small piece of black stone of any variety. Wrap the paper around the stone, and tie it with a piece of black string, ribbon, or leather thong. Recite the incantation of Erasure, and drop the stone into the jar. Seal the jar, adding a black or red wax seal if you wish. Set the finished Jar aside in an out of the way place. You may choose to devote further intention upon the working by shaking it each night for a given number of days. You may also choose to bury it.

Should you wish at some point to reverse this operation, begin by opening the Jar and pouring out the liquid. Remove the glyph from the stone, and dry the paper in the sun. If you do not wish to keep the stone, cast it into running water.

Black Ice

Black Ice magic is a technique largely analogous, if opposite in elemental polarity, to candle magic. It can be applied either as an irreversible act of Erasure, or conversely, to free oneself from a curse, binding, or other baleful sending that one might be suffering from. To create the ice itself, simply prepare and freeze a cube of Black Water.

If you wish to perform a potent banishment on an adversarial entity or concept, scribe their symbol on the ice with a scratch awl or similar tool. When constructing this figure, keep in mind that the action is very similar to carving on soft stone. Linear strokes are easier to execute than curved ones. Place the cube in a cup, small cauldron, or other vessel on your altar. As the ice melts, their presence, influence, and potency are likewise eradicated. Once the ice has melted, allow the resulting black melt water to evaporate. This phase change from solid to liquid to gaseous form serves to eradicate the target's power. This working is not easily undone, and should be reserved for use against particularly undesirable forces.

If you wish to free yourself from unwanted influence or constraint, in which you are in effect frozen, write your personal glyph on a small piece of paper. Roll it up tightly and bind it with black thread.. Freeze this miniature scroll into a cube of black ice. Place it on your altar as described above. As the ice melts away, you will be freed from your unwanted circumstance. Unroll your paper and lay it out to dry on your altar. Desecrate and discard the liquid as you see fit.

Deep Diving

Once you have reached a level of comfort and familiarity with the concept of dissolution through unaided meditation and visualization, there is a more advanced technique that you may wish to experiment with. The practice of reaching an altered state of consciousness via sensory deprivation and potentially restriction of movement lends itself well to meditating on the Void. It is a simple, yet effective way of forcing the mind to focus on something other than the body and its stimulatory relationship with its environment. When physical sensory input is restricted, the mind is freed from the distraction of processing their input. This technique has been used in numerous faiths and traditions, both ancient and modern.

There are a number of possible ways to achieve this physical state, some more accessible than others. The so-called Witches' Cradle is of particular interest for this purpose. As described by Raymond Buckland in his Complete Book of Witchcraft, it is essentially a heavyweight body sack or wrapping that is suspended vertically to facilitate disorientation via swinging. It is not difficult to assemble a similar rig, albeit horizontally oriented, via the use of hoods, sleep sacks, and swings that are commercially available from fetish gear suppliers. The use of such equipment for this purpose requires the aid of a trusted and preferably competent and experienced assistant for getting into and out of the Cradle, as well to monitor you for any emergencies or unforeseen circumstances that may occur. Be cautious and be smart in the use of this method. I recommend starting with very short sessions in order to familiarize yourself with the sensation of restriction. This is obviously not an activity for anyone prone to claustrophobia. If you are hesitant to commit to such a level of restriction from the beginning, you can wrap yourself up in a blanket to get your body used to the sensation.

In my experience, the absolute best environment for deep diving the self is the sensory deprivation of a floatation tank. This apparatus was devised by the American physician and neuroscientist John Lilly. It consists of a concentrated solution of skin-temperature magnesium sulfate (Epsom salt) combined with darkness and silence. The buoyancy and thermal neutrality provided by the solution allows for a profound dissolution of the ability to perceive where one stops and one's environment begins. It is a natural physical precursor to the desired mental state that is the goal of this exercise.

Once ensconced in your selected method of deprivation, take your time acclimating to it. Relax and focus on your breathing, and allow the natural dissociation to proceed. Eventually, you will achieve a floating and lightly dissociative sensation. At this point, turn your thoughts inward. Do not fear the darkness behind your eyes, but rather dive deep into it. Embrace it and integrate your conscious with it. Seek downward and inward, until you penetrate its veil and reach the luminous spark at the core of your existence.

Once you have arrived at this state, envision the bright mote of your awareness spreading out as a luminous, translucent sphere through the darkness, encompassing it within the construct of yourself. This can continue for an arbitrary length of time, which itself will quickly come to be very fluid within this state. As your sphere of focus grows, it dims to match the darkness, and yet is not subsumed by it.

Once your expansion reaches a desired point of equilibrium, allow yourself to simply breathe and be and open yourself to the stillness of the Void. The boundary between yourself and the greater universe will begin to waver, as it is revealed for the illusion that it is. As in the Disintegration rite, your consciousness will become diffuse, and yet all-encompassing. You and the Void will be as one. You will be omnipresent and unassailable. You may have visions, as when scrying. They may be revelational or even terrible at first, as your mind unloads its baggage. These will pass, and you will reach a state of luxurious calm. Draw vitality and satiety from this dark and peaceful place. If you feel that you have drawn the attention of any proto forms by your presence, do not be alarmed. They cannot act against you unless you first engage them and quicken them by your own expenditure of attention. Ignore them.

When it is time to end your session, construct a new

Voidworking

boundary in order to demarcate yourself from all else, just as the Ouroboros divides order from chaos. Perceive the luminous sphere at it begins to coalesce once more. Begin to contract your consciousness and focus back into your body. As you do so, draw down and concentrate a mote of the Void into yourself, a minute matte black sphere harbored as one might a shield a candle flame between the palms of one's hands. This mote can be used in further workings as a link to the greater Void, for indeed it is without scale, and one iota of it is as its entirety, in accordance with Hermetic principles. If you are performing another rite or meditation, let your encapsulation of this Void microcosm aid you in achieving a greater degree of connection to the greater whole .

If you have not properly conditioned yourself via the less strenuous practices previously described to the rigors of interacting so directly with the Void, you may find that keeping this mote within you will begin to drain you rather than enhancing your work. If it thus becomes necessary to divest yourself of it, visualize it again, and then speak these words:

"I relinquish this seed of nothingness. It is returned to Void whence it came."

Regardless of the chosen method of sensory deprivation, there is the possibility of enhancing the state of openness via the use of various entheogenic substances. Unfortunately, many of these may be unlawful in some locations, so there is an additional risk involved in their use. If you do choose to enhance your experience in this manner, do so cautiously and respectfully of the substances used. Don't consider using them until you have some experience in sensory deprivation without them. Too, do not use any substances in a deprivation and restriction practice until you are thoroughly familiar with their effects and duration in a more casual environment. If you feel that a substance may be detrimental to your dive, then do not use it. These materials are tools, just as any other. They should always be used in a complementary manner which benefits a working. They are not for playing ego games with, at least not in the context of this technique.

Distilling the Static

One of the immensely powerful forces of the Universe is the *black hole*. This is a compact yet super-massive celestial structure that can be created, among other ways, when a very large star collapses in on itself at the end of its life cycle. A black hole is a *blackbody*, or a physical structure which absorbs all of the radiation that strikes it, reflecting none. In addition, the immense mass of the black hole affects the space around itself such that it creates a gravitational vortex and draws matter towards itself like water swirling down the drain. For obvious reasons, this structure can be thought of as an example of the Void in our own Universe. As such, the black hole can be a useful concept for constructing a technique for the gathering of ambient energy from your surrounding environment, in effect harvesting and distilling the static of the noosphere for whatever purpose you desire.

Stand erect with your arms outstretched at your sides, with hands facing forward cruciform-style. Close your eyes. Take several long, deep breaths. Make yourself aware of your personal energy field. Some may also refer to this as a qi field or even an aura. The term is not as important as the concept, that each living being is surrounded and permeated by a unique energy field that can be manipulated through practice and focus to various ends. This has been referred to by many names, such as the Greek *pneuma* and the Proto-Indo-European root word **aiw*. Determine the color and nature of your personal field as you see fit. Take inspiration from kirlian photography, or whatever your association of such a phenomenon is. In actuality, the biophotonic radiance of a human body is quite faint and tends to be in the red end of the spectrum, but you should not let this limit your visualization. If you close your eyes and in your mind, you are surrounded with 10 feet of blue flames and lightning, use that imagery.

However, it is so visualized, project your field to its full extent, and hold it there blazing outward for a few beats. Sweep your arms down and your hands together in front of a spot just below your navel, so they are flat against your abdomen, one hand over another. As you do so, feel your field contract to a single point at your center of gravity. This point exerts a strong pull on the free energy around you. It will begin to spiral inward and ultimately be subsumed by your focal point. As you absorb it, you naturally entrain it to your own frequency, and claim it as your own. Once you have as much as you need, envision the point growing back outward into an expanding wave that returns your surrounding field to its original shape, but of a greater intensity due to the energy that you have added to it. This augmentation may be used for imbuing talismans, healing, feeding servitors, or any other purpose desired.

Condenser glyph

If you wish to store your excess energy, you can create a *condenser*. This is a small slip of paper with a glyph marked on it that you feed into by holding it between your hands and projecting the energy that you have accumulated. This can then be placed on your altar or kept in a safe place until a need arises that warrants its use. This construct is analogous to a capacitor in an electrical circuit. In order to release the power imbued in the glyph, hold the paper in the closed fist of your receptive hand. Bring your fist up to your mouth, as if to cover a cough. Inhale deeply, drawing air through your fist, flowing past the condenser. Envision the stored energy being drawn into you as you inhale. The slip of paper should be burned afterwards rather than reused.

The Veil of Shadows

Working within a paradigm that evokes a sense of darkness and shadow, it is only natural that one application of such a discipline would be concealment, either physical or metaphysical. In the latter case, whether it is from other magical practitioners or some other entity, you can disappear entirely from their perception. I've referred to this process previously in terms of "dimming the flame" to keep from being perceived by whatever faculty is that applies here. That is in itself a good question, how is it that operant magical entities "feel" one-another? Some aspects of Bohm's *Implicate Order* theory that I investigated in *Quantum Sorcery* might explain it, but regardless of how it operates, it is extra-sensory in nature and thus more easily influenced than a more mundane faculty. In terms of physical concealment, it is possible by application of this technique to make someone simply overlook your presence. As with all workings it will take practice and refinement to achieve success.

Again, envision yourself standing on the plain of purest matte black. Rather than sinking into its surface, the surface slowly rises and envelops you in a veil of dark shadow. The exact form is left to your personal taste, whether it is more akin to a fog bank, a pair of enfolding wings, or a second skin. This extension of the Void relies semantically on a blackbody nature to absorb all observational energy, such that none is scattered or reflected. Pull your projected sense of self inward and downward. If you are in actual close proximity to the one you wish to avoid, ensure that you do not directly look at them, and especially avoid the possibility of eye contact. The effectiveness of this technique can be uncanny when properly executed.

To discontinue this suppression, simply envision your presence rising and expanding, and the veil receding from you and back into the null surface from which it emanated. The overall process can be augmented by symbols, gestures, or incantations if desired, but these are as always completely optional.

Scrying: Gazing into the Void

The practice of scrying in general is ancient, and is one of the most fundamental acts of practical magic. By scrying, a sorcerer attempts to get a glimpse at the future, or to gain insight on a situation in the present. The basic premise is to concentrate one's visual focus on some type of object, often a reflective glass or liquid surface in order to enter a receptive mind state in which messages or visions can be received. Depending on one's paradigm, these visions may be thought to emerge from the subconscious mind, or they may be bestowed by an external higher power. Whichever source is attributed as the origin of this ability, the result is the same. The images received may be highly subjective and require interpretation within the context of the questions in the mind of the seer. Free-form scrying, without a predisposition is also possible. This is a stream-of consciousness exercise that may yield chaotic imagery of varying quality or applicability, but it can serve as a useful practice for honing one's skills of reception and interpretation.

When scrying I often employ, a highly polished obsidian disk. I focus my gaze intently upon it, until it begins to unfocus of its own accord, and all but the stone fall into the background of perception. I wait until images, usually fleeting, start to appear. I make note of them, but do not attempt to contextualize them until the stream of images trails off. I keep a notebook close at hand to record what I saw and to try and discern their meaning. Images don't always appear, and even if they do, I can't always make sense of them. Rather than ascribing a supernatural origin to this phenomenon, I trend towards the materialist point of view, and assume that the images are bubbling up from my subconscious mind. The mirror allows for a distraction of the conscious mind that can help the forms get through. In my experience, if there is something that is trying to manifest just past the edge of conscious perception, it can be nudged across that threshold to a space where it can be known. Often, the images and impressions are not immediately useful or applicable to what I am seeking insight on, but in many cases I have found that they make sense at a future point in time.

The physical medium itself is not as important as appropriate technique and mindset are. A black glass or obsidian sphere may be used, so may a blackened glass mirror or a bowl of Black Water. Whatever the case, the surface acts as a focus by which you can bypass the static that I have previously discussed, resulting in the desired effect. Black mirror scrying in this manner is symbolic of gazing into the Void itself. The visions that you will see are proto-forms of situations that may come to pass, or may already have. The act of scrying itself brings to bear the larger question of sorcery in general, namely how much the magician directs the formation of the future from what is seen and interpreted, as opposed to merely passively observing a die that is already cast.

The tradition of using an obsidian mirror is probably best known from the Enochian workings of John Dee and Edward Kelly. A small mirror that is claimed to have belonged to Dee is held by the British Museum, but there is a question as to its authenticity. A modern substitute can be found in any smartphone screen. It is also easy enough to construct a black mirror from a photo frame. Simply remove the glass from the frame and paint one side black with spray paint. Replace the glass with the unpainted side facing out. If desired, a border script may be inscribed around the edges of the face.

The basic technique for scrying is simple. The room should be dimly lit. Candlelight is particularly appropriate. Perform a basic banishing if it feels appropriate to you. It's not necessary, but it can help set your mindset for the work to come. Sit in a comfortable position with your implement on a flat surface in front of you. If you're using a flat object, such as a mirror or bowl of black water, try placing a candle on the far side of it from you. The flickering light can help stimulate the process. If you're using a glass or obsidian sphere, the light source is better placed next to you. Stare intently at your surface, then allow your eyes to unfocus, without moving your gaze. Still your mind, using one of the Void meditation techniques. Sit in silence, and wait for images to appear. If you get no results, try again later. This is not a practice than can be forced. When an image or stream of them has concluded, record your results by whatever means you see fit. A written description, sketch, or a voice recording are all worthwhile methods. It can be useful to cross-reference the results of different sessions to see if there is an emergent form that manifests piece-meal.

The Last: Contemplating Death

The most absurd thing about life is that it ends. We all die. Coming to grips with this is something that we have a lifetime, however long that may be, to do. But most sentient beings likely never do. It's not something that we tend to want to consider until the moments that we must, at the inevitable end of our existence. In fact, one study has reached the conclusion that we are prone to denying our own mortality at a very deep psychological level. There may be an evolutionary advantage in this behavior that assisted our early ancestors in being willing to take the necessary risks to find an appropriate mate. It may be possible through rigorous discipline to override this tendency, but for most people, it is ingrained. I believe that there is value in undertaking the development of willful mastery over this mechanism, and I feel that there is comfort to be found in contemplating and accepting our fate, rather than living in fear of the inevitable.

American actor Harry Dean Stanton summarized this perfectly in an interview he gave at age 87, four years before his death:

The void, the concept of nothingness, is terrifying to most people on the planet. And I get anxiety attacks myself. I know the fear of that void. You have to learn to die before you die. You give up, surrender to the void, to nothingness.

There is a change in one's point of view that occurs when one reaches a certain point in life and realizes that more days have probably been lived than there are yet to live. This shift may immediately follow a brush with mortality, such as a catastrophic injury or the sudden onset of a serious illness. It may also occur naturally as part of a so-called mid-life crisis. Regardless of how the realization is reached, the thought will never again be completely put out of mind from that moment onward. This need not be a cause for despair. It is not morbid, but rather simply wise to begin to explore the nature of non-existence.

Several of the techniques that I've described, such as The Attributes of the Void mantra and the Disintegration method can assist in this effort. If you desire a more structured esoteric model for understanding the process of death, there are a number of effective systems that can be of benefit, even without believing in the underlying religious systems from which they originate.

The *Bardo Thodol* is a text of the Nyingma school of Tibetan Buddhism. Although it is most commonly known in the

West as the *Tibetan Book of the Dead*. This text is concerned with the liberation of the self from the cycle of rebirth through a description of the transitions between the intermediate states of existence that lie between death and rebirth. The soul is thought to encounter a cavalcade of divine beings, both benevolent and malevolent. The latter will judge and even dismember the soul. Although horrific in appearance, this process is actually a necessary alchemical refinement and purification of the self. The ultimate goal of this process of atonement and distillation of essence is to escape the cycle of rebirth, and the transition to a higher state of existence. The passages of the book are intended to be read to one who is dying, or who has very recently died.

Another structure can be found in what is commonly the *Egyptian Book of the Dead*, but should be more accurately named the *Book of Life*. It consists of a set of spells that are designed to assist the soul through its passage into the afterlife. This required the memorization of myriad names of objects and deities that must be passed by the soul. Traditionally, such a text was uniquely assembled for the use of an individual who had the wherewithal to afford it. A modern equivalent can be researched and assembled from the extant examples that have survived. In contrast to the *Bardo Thodol*, the Egyptian incantations are intended to be used by the dead soul itself.

A likely more familiar approach is the personification of Death in the form of the Grim Reaper. This scythe-wielding skeletal figure in black robes appears in nearly every form of media. The Reaper fulfills the role of a *psychopomp*, or guide who helps convey the dead soul to their ultimate fate. In this context, it would be to facilitate the return to the Void rather than any given realm of reward or punishment. The Reaper is a remarkably easy symbol to work with for initiating a conversation with. Simply pick your favorite incarnation of the character, and visualize sitting down in a comforting location to discuss your inevitable meeting with them. If this particular embodiment is not workable for you, there are myriad other entities that can be evoked for their guidance. Hermes himself is one of these, as are Anubis, Azrael, Charon the ferryman on the river Styx, and the Valkyries of Norse mythology who choose the slain for the halls of Odin and Freyja. Every culture in every time has a being or category of beings that serve this purpose in their mythos. There are also contemporary embodiments to be found in popular media that may be more easily co-opted for your purpose. As I've stated before, the ostensibly "low" origins of these modern fictions do not make them any less valid.

Although most often portrayed as male, Death is genderless unless you assign it one in your image of it. A strong female portrayal can be found in *Santa Muerte*, the Mexican folk saint. She has a rich body of myth and ritual associated with her that can be used to reach an understanding of her nature and function. The character of Death in Neil Gaiman's *Sandman* comic series is another widely-known female personification.

It is in contemplation of the process of the death of the

psyche and ostensible progress of the soul that the truest nature of the Void is revealed. It is not a construct of destruction, rather of creation, potential and renewal. Its oblivion should not be approached with a sense of fear, but calm. Cosmologically and mythologically it seems that nothing always precedes something. In utter absence, presence emerges. Whether in the sense of the renewal of the world after Ragnarok, or in the cycles of cosmic death and rebirth in the ekpyrotic universe model, creation occurs from the seeming dissolution of all. If the universe is approaching a heat death, then we can surmise that something will ultimately come forth from its vacuum. It must.

Conclusion

It is not surprising in these present times of global societal unrest, climate change, and pandemic infection that the Void is experiencing a surge of memetic popularity. It is a stand-in for the sum of our unknown fears. This negative aspect is needless and counterproductive. The Void is not evil, hungry, or even sentient. It is the wellspring of utmost potential that precedes all creation, and there is a great deal of magical power and utility to be found in its boundless expanse. Even though its ultimate nature transcends human understanding, we can eradicate irrational fears through developing a level of comfort and familiarity with the aspects of it that we *can* grasp. There is great power to be found in the nullification of fear.

In myth and legend, it is the purview of the gods to bring forth order from the primordial state, but this can serve as the inspiration for similar acts of creation by we mere mortals. We are all in effect children of the Void, and thus the inheritors of its potential. It is my hope that this work has provided you with a greater understanding of the Void, as well as the techniques to parley this insight into increasing the effectiveness of your own magical practice. Let your fear of this inevitable destination of life's journey be dispelled, for it was also the ultimate source of all existence. From there we came, and to there we must also return, both singularly and collectively. This is simply part of the great cycle that governs over all. Secure in this knowledge, go forth and work your Will as you see fit.

Io ION! Vargr23 NmNoNtNl.

Sources Consulted

Black Magic
Aquino, Michael A. 2002.

Imajica
Barker, Clive. HarperCollins e-books. Kindle Edition 2002.

T. A. Z. The Temporary Autonomous Zone, Ontological Anarchy, Poetic Terrorism
Bey, Hakim   Autonomedia,   1985.

The Bible, King James, Book 1: Genesis
http://www.gutenberg.org/cache/epub/8001/pg8001-images.html
Accessed 4/27/2019.

Buckland's Complete Book of Witchcraft
Buckland, Raymond. Llewellyn Publications, 1986.

Liber Null & Psychonaut
Carroll, Peter. Samuel Weiser, 1987.

Void Magick
Chaote, Thomas.
archive.org/details/VoidMagick/page/n9
Accessed 11/3/2018.

The Phenomenon of Man
de Chardin, Teilhard.   Tr. by Bernard Wall,   Harper and

Row, 1959.
The Confessions of Aleister Crowley
Crowley, Aleister, Penguin, 1989.

Liber Aba: Book 4, Part III - Magick in Theory and Practice
Crowley, Aleister
hermetic.com/crowley/book-4/aba3
Accessed 10/12/2018.

"Anaximander," by Dirk L. Couprie, *The Internet Encyclopedia of Philosophy, ISSN 2161-0002.*
https://www.iep.utm.edu
Accessed 7/13/2019.

Dibitettoa, Giuseppe, Petri, Nicol`o and Schillo, Marjorie
Nothing really matters
https://arxiv.org/pdf/2002.01764.pdf
Accessed 3/6/2020.

Rig Veda, tr. by Ralph T.H. Griffith, [1896], at sacred-texts.com
www.sacred-texts.com/hin/rigveda/rv10129.htm
Accessed 8/4/2018.

Tao Te Ching
Lao Tzu
translated by John Chalmers (1868)
www.bopsecrets.org/gateway/passages/tao-te-ching.htm
Accessed 3/31/2019.

Majjhima Nikaya 121 - *Cula-Sunnata Sutta - The Lesser*

Discourse on Emptiness
From: *"A Treasury of the Buddha's Words"* (Discourses from the Middle Collection); translated by Ven. Nyanamoli Thera; edited by Phra Khantipalo, Wat Bovoranives Vihara, Bangkok, Thailand
Mahamakut Rajavidyalaya Press; 287 Phra Sumeru Road; Bangkok 2, Thailand; 1977
www.budsas.org/ebud/ebsut016.htm
Accessed 7/19/2018.

Inflationary Universe: A possible solution to the horizon and flatness problems, Guth, Alan, Physical Review D Volume 23, Number 2, 15 January 1981.

The Babylonian Genesis - The Story of Creation, second edition
Heildel, Alexander
University of Chicago Press, 1963.

The Theogony of Hesiod
translated by Hugh G. Evelyn-White, [1914], at sacred-texts.com
www.sacred-texts.com/cla/hesiod/theogony.htm
Accessed 8/4/2018.

The Poetic Edda
translated by Lee M. Hollander
University of Texas Press; Second edition, Revised 1986.

Conceptions of God in Ancient Egypt: The One and the Many
Hornung, Erik translated by John Baines, Cornell University Press 1982.

Dave Smith

Hues of the Void
dishonored.fandom.com/wiki/Hues_of_the_Void,_by_A._Nongui
Accessed 9/3/2019.

The Call of Cthulhu
Lovecraft, Howard Phillips 1926
In: *Black Seas of Infinity: The Best of H.P. Lovecraft*
Selected by Andrew Wheeler
SFBC Science Fiction, Garden City, New York, 2001.

Through the Gates of the Silver Key
Lovecraft, Howard Phillip and Price, E. Hoffmann 1934
en.wikisource.org/wiki/Through_the_Gates_of_the_Silver_Key/full
Accessed 3/31/2019.

Ancient History Encyclopedia: Egyptian Book of the Dead
Mark, Joshua K., March 24, 2016.
www.ancient.eu/Egyptian_Book_of_the_Dead
Accessed 9/21/2019.

POP MAGIC!
Morrison, Grant
In: *Book of Lies: The Disinformation Guide to Magick and the Occult*
edited by Richard Metzger
Disinformation Company, 2003.

Beyond Good and Evil: Prelude to a Philosophy of the Future
Nietzsche, Friedrich. Penguin Classics, 1990.

Internet Encyclopedia of Philosophy: Nihilism
Pratt, Alan
www.iep.utm.edu/nihilism/
Accessed 11/30/2018.

Proto-Indo-European Etyma, Linguistics Research Center,
University of Texas at Austin
lrc.la.utexas.edu/lex/semantic/field/BP_YG
Accessed 1/25/2020.

Your Brain 'Shields' Itself from the Existential Threat of Death
Saplakoglu, Yasemin
www.livescience.com/brain-shields-idea-death.html
Accessed 10/26/2019.

The Zen of Harry Dean Stanton: 'Surrender to The Void, To Nothingness'
Sorene, Paul, September 17, 2017
www.flashbak.com/the-zen-of-harry-dean-stanton-surrender-to-the-void-to-nothingness-386512/
Accessed 9/21/2019.

The Book of Pleasure (Self-Love)
Spare, Austin Osman, 93 Publishing, 1913. (1975 Edition).

About the Author

Frequently known as Vargr23 among online and magical communities, Dave Smith has been studying and practicing magic in various forms for over 30 years. He was the founder of the Grove of Oakhaven, the Lawspeaker of the Northstar Kindred, and a founding elder of the Indiana Asatru Council. His articles and reviews have appeared in the journals Konton and Idunna, as well as on his website SpikeVision (www.spikevision.org).

He has indulged his lifelong love of information by working in a science library, an astronomical observatory, and as a data architect. Along the way, he has also been a brewer, leatherworker, performance artist, and sideshow crewman.

He graduated from Indiana State University in 1993, and currently lives in Indianapolis, Indiana.

Other Titles by Dave Smith:

Quantum Sorcery: The Science of Chaos Magic, Second edition, 2009.

Recent Titles from Megalithica Books

Coming Forth by Day by Storm Constantine

This book explores the myths of Ancient Egyptian gods and goddesses – showing how their stories relate to aspects of our lives, hopes and aspirations, and how we can learn from these ancient narratives. Through 28 deep and evocative pathworkings and rituals, the author provides a rich and vivid system of magic that the practitioner – whether experienced or a novice – can utilize in the search for self-knowledge, and to help themselves, others and the world around them. ISBN: 978-1-912241-11-8 Price: £12.99, $16.99

SHE: Primal Meetings with the Dark Goddess by Storm Constantine & Andrew Collins

The Dark Goddess is unpredictable, dispassionate, cruel, and often deadly. She reflects our deepest desires, fears, hopes and expectations. In this fully-illustrated book, Storm Constantine and Andrew Collins have selected a fascinating range of 34 goddesses, including some who are not so well-known. The pathworkings to meet them and explore their realms will offer insight into these often-misunderstood deities. (This title is also available as a limited edition, numbered hardback.) ISBN: 978-1-912241-06-4 Price: £12.99, $18.99

My First Book of Magic by Dolores Ashcroft-Nowicki

I want to tell you how the Pagan Way works, what it does, and how it makes you feel. I want you to know the joy this oldest of all traditions can bring you. The way of sharing it with humans, elementals, sprites, animals, plants, trees, and of course other pagans.

If you have a child in your life that has the look of far memory in their eyes, gift them with this guide. If you remember the child you were, read this book and reopen the gates of your wonder." – Ivo Dominguez Jr., author of 'Keys to Perception'.

ISBN: 978-1-912241-10-1 Price: £10.99, $15.99

www.immanion-press.com

www.ingramcontent.com/pod-product-compliance
Lightning Source LLC
LaVergne TN
LVHW041300080426
835510LV00009B/809